Up & Running
The Journey Continues

BARVENIA WOOTEN

WWW.SELFPUBLISHN30DAYS.COM

Published by Self Publish -N- 30 Days

Copyright 2019 Barvenia Wooten.

All rights reserved worldwide. No part of this book may be reproduced or transmitted in any form or by any means electronic or mechanical, including photocopying, recording or by any information storage and retrieval system without written permission from Barvenia Wooten.

Printed in the United States of America

ISBN: 978-1-70867-977-4

1. Autobiography 2. Success 3. Women 4. Sports 5. Coaching

Barvenia Wooten Up & Running: The Journey Continues

Disclaimer/Warning:
This book is intended for lecture and informative purposes only. This publication is designed to provide competent and reliable information regarding the subject matter covered. The author or publisher are not engaged in rendering legal or professional advice. Laws vary from state to state and if legal, financial, or other expert assistance is needed, the services of a professional should be sought. The author and publisher disclaim any liability that is incurred from the use or application of the contents of this book.

I dedicate this book to my mom and to those who continue to seek their truth, their purpose for living. I believe there is greatness in all of us.

"Ask, and it shall be given you; Seek, and you shall find; Knock and it shall be opened unto you."
MATTHEW 7:7

Barvenia

Table Of Contents

Introduction — 1

1. The Streets Of Cincinnati — 5
2. My New Best Friend — 25
3. The Halls Of High School — 37
4. Destined To Make A Difference — 59
5. My Ticket Out — 81
6. The Pursuit Of Balance — 103
7. Dreams Do Come True — 119
8. A Spiritual Awakening & Revelation — 141
9. The Journey Continues — 155

INTRODUCTION

I am excited about the opportunity to write my own story. Where do I start? The yearning to do something great with my life, as far as I can remember, resonated deep within my soul. I have always wanted to make a difference in life. The determination and willingness to persevere in the face of adversity has always motivated me to fulfill my dreams and achieve my goals.

It all started on that beautiful day of September 25, 1961, when the stars aligned and I became the fourth child born of the Reverend Leathea Wooten Burden and the second set of children of the late Cornelius Williams. I'm not sure where to begin, but all I know is that I can remember back as early as five years old that I was here to accomplish great things with my life. I always knew that God was with me and was present in my life.

Growing up in Cincinnati, Ohio, my mother moved around a lot, with each move being within a five to ten mile radius. I would later find out that she had to move often because many times she didn't have enough money to pay the rent. By the time I finished sixth grade, I had already attended six different elementary schools.

At that time, it was not known that moving and changing schools so often could very well have a negative effect on the cognitive development of children throughout their formative years. I recall having challenges with language and speaking with clarity. Nevertheless, I always knew that I was destined to make something out of myself.

I was an active child and was always involved in extracurricular activities from childhood through college. I was impressionable and I was always eager and excited to learn. I discovered that I had a true passion for life. With my determination to be my best at everything I did, I continually found a way to excel despite my challenges. And thus, against all odds, my journey has been both edifying and enlightening.

I believe that the lessons I have learned from my experiences on my journey will provide others with the motivation and inspiration to overcome obstacles and challenges that many of us will face as we continue to seek and prayerfully discover our purpose. My experiences on this journey have taught me valuable lessons along the way.

The lessons that I learned from my mother and my mentors were priceless. Their words of wisdom helped me throughout my trials and triumphs on my journey. The most important lesson that I embraced has been to never give up. There were many times that I struggled with being labeled an overachiever. One moment everyone was cheering me on and the next, those same people were saying unkind things about me. This paradoxical behavior clearly didn't make sense to me. However, over time, I found a way to deal with it. I found solace in music and my faith.

I'm always intrigued when I read other people's stories. It's very interesting to see how they overcame their challenges and how their lives have evolved. It is my hope that as you read my story, it invigorates and inspires you to continue your journey intentionally and on purpose. It is no coincidence that you are reading my book.

All of us have a meaning and purpose in life and it is to constantly ask the question, "Why Am I Here?" "What is my dharma, my purpose?" I am constantly reminded of the Scripture that says, "Ask, and it shall be given you; Seek, and you shall find; Knock, and it shall be opened unto you" (Matthew 7:7, KJV).

As we continue to search for the truth of our soul, I believe that the answers come in different ways. God, the Divine, is always speaking to us. It is up to us to learn to be still and quiet ourselves in prayer and meditation. I believe that by going within, we can find the truth of our souls, our reason for being.

I have always felt an intuitive connection with a higher power, God, the Divine. This power has been present in my life as longer as I can remember. The freedom to express myself is the driving force that has sustained me. It has given me the strength and courage to become the person that I am today. Come take this journey with me as I share my thoughts and experiences in hopes that you, too, will "bear witness to your journey back to your connection with the Divine" as you experience this thing called life.

Chapter 1
THE STREETS OF CINCINNATI

Born during the '60s, the Motown era, the civil rights era and the awaking of my soul, it was my time to come. Discussion years later with a dear friend about how we were born left me with a new understanding and realization of the possible significance of my birth. I shared with her that I was born a breech baby; bottom first. Then my friend enlightened me and said that because I was born bottom down, I have been showing my bottom (self) ever since. I laughed and the thought made me smile. Metaphorically speaking, she was right.

My name "Barvenia" is unique. At the time of my birth, my mother's two best girlfriends wanted her to name me after them. After much consideration as to not offend them, she decided to combine both of their names, Barbara and Luvenia. And thus, created Barvenia. Over time, I realized that my mother in her own wisdom, knew that I would be the one amongst my siblings to achieve great things and be the one that she could count on. My half siblings have common names. Linda, my only sister, the oldest, two older brothers, Carlos and Anthony, and my younger brother and only full sibling, Alan. I believe am the chosen one of the family. Destined to succeed.

Growing up in Cincinnati during the '60s was a fascinating time for me.

I can remember how exciting and fun it was to play up and down the streets of several neighbors where I lived. Listening to the Motown era music, living and breathing the Civil Rights Movement, participating in the local sports clubs and organizations, life for me was wonderful.

Of the six different elementary schools that I attended before moving on to junior high school, three of them, South Avondale Elementary, Burton Elementary and most profoundly, Rothenberg Elementary, would contribute significantly to my development and growth. They set the foundation for what was to come.

> In that moment, I didn't understand the impact that Dr. King's life would have on my own life.

My first school, South Avondale Elementary, is where I attended second grade when the news came that Dr. Martin Luther King, Jr. was assassinated. I remember our class walking outside carrying signs, but I don't remember what they said. I can only imagine what they said: "Peace & Love," "They Killed Him," "Dr. King, We Shall Overcome," just to name a few. It was a sad day. In that moment, I didn't understand the impact that Dr. King's life would have on my own life. I surely didn't understand how influential and meaningful Dr. King's work would be for me as I journeyed outside of my community.

My mother never discussed with us the difference of our skin color until later in life. We were never taught to hate another person, regardless of their race, ethnicity or creed. I believe my mom tried to shelter us from the racism and discrimination that I'm sure she faced every day. I can't imagine how much she had to endure.

Over the next few years, my awareness of these differences became more real and alive; things became black or white, no in-between. There were neighborhoods that we were forbidden to go in and places that did not welcome blacks. This was my introduction to the awareness that I was living in two different worlds simultaneously and thus, adhered to my mom's words. The world was not as homogeneous as I thought.

Despite this new awareness, I was still in touch with my joy for life. Chaos and riots were happening around me and yet it had no effect on me until later. Even though I witnessed these events taking place, somehow, I managed to move forward as if it wasn't happening. Life was good to me. It was as if I was protected while living in my own world, even as I lived within this newfound different world.

As I look back, I believe my guardian angels have been protecting me since my birth. Nevertheless, the lesson that I learned during this time would leave me questioning the very existence of my life as a black girl. A black girl that grew up in a world that seemed cruel and full of racism and discrimination just because of the color of her skin.

The music we listened to told the stories of life as a black person living in America. The music had meaning and it was empowering. I know that this was the time that I was supposed to be born. My soul resonated with the music and social changes that were evolving within the black community. I learned a lot about myself through music as a black person growing up in a world that didn't value other cultures. Many people (activists) lost their lives fighting for equal rights and the fair treatment of blacks in America. Even today I still find myself asking, "Was Dr. King's fight for justice and equality in vain?"

The movement of social change was real and I was in it. The journey was happening. Despite the constant struggles that I faced being black, I wanted to be alive. The energy was high and contagious. I wanted everyone that I encountered to feel alive and experience this energy. I found myself always encouraging and inspiring my friends not only to follow their dreams, but also to get involved in the movement. Being outside and in nature allowed me to feel the presence of God within me. I knew I was destined for greatness. When I take the time to look back and reflect on my life, it's amazing to see how far I have come and evolved.

As I reflect on the Civil Rights Movement during high school, the significance of Dr. King and the movement would leave an indelible mark on the rest of my life, even up to now. I was able to see how important his life was and how I wanted to help carry on his legacy. Dr. King dreamt of a world where people would not be judged by the color of their skin, but the content of their character. I yearned to do my part and contribute to Dr. King's dream. What a beautiful world it would be to see his dream come to light.

Every year I looked forward to learning more about Dr. King, reading books on his life, attending many events that celebrated his life and often listening to his speeches. I discovered that Dr. King had visited Virginia Union University, which would one day be my alma mater, before his passing. In Chapter 5 I will have the pleasure sharing my personal experience with his wife, Coretta Scott King.

This was an era when being "black and proud," lyrics from the king of soul, James Brown, vibrated throughout our communities and neighborhoods. We wore Afros and dashikis. It was a great time to experience feeling comfortable in my black skin. The talent shows and plays that I participated in allowed me to express myself freely without judgment. I enjoyed every event and show because it brought me joy. It provided me the stage to perform without fear and trepidation since we usually performed in groups.

The support from the group helped build my confidence and increased my social skills. I had grown stronger and more determined to be my best. Strength and determination became my rock.

The second school, Burton Elementary, is where I attended the third grade. Although I was shy, I recall participating in a lot of school events including talent shows. We were encouraged to be proud of our black skin and our natural hair.

The majority of my experiences at Burton Elementary were positive except for this one incident that would remain with me for the rest of my life. As I sat at my table doing my work, one of my teachers hit me hard in the back of my head for no apparent reason. I'm unsure as to why. I felt hurt and ashamed. What caused this action?

For some strange reason, I didn't tell my mother. I am unsure if I was scared to tell my mother, fearing how she might handle the situation. Maybe I was fearful that if my teacher found out that I had told my mother, she might deny the situation and treat me unkindly. This situation left a bad memory in my mind. Even until this day, I have been working on forgiveness and trying to understand why it happened.

I realized later that this experience played a major role in my inability to speak up for myself early in my life. Despite this encounter, I was able to deal with the situation and move forward. Along my journey, I somehow found the strength and didn't allow events like this to hinder or stop me. I surged forward using sports as my outlet and refuge. Nevertheless, Burton Elementary had instilled in me many core values that were instrumental in shaping my character as a child. Knowing what I know now, I should have told my mother.

I believe that God puts angels all around to guide and protect us, our guardian angels. Some you can see; some you can only feel and some you know are there at your call. One of my angels was my fourth-grade gym teacher, Mr. Schumacher, at Rothenberg Elementary School. This was the third of the six elementary schools that would profoundly change my life and open a world for me beyond my imagination. Once again, my mother had moved and my younger brother, Alan Wooten, and I had to start another school.

Mr. Schumacher welcomed my brother and me to the new school and presented us with a gift of knockers. During that time, knockers were very popular. They were two large marbles tied to the end of two strings attached to a handle. The object of the knockers was to strategically swing the marbles so that they would touch each other in a rhythmic motion. We were both excited about the gift. I remember competing with my brother to see whose knockers could last the longest before the marbles missed each other and came to a stop. I believe I always won.

Mr. Schumacher took a special interest in my brother and me. He was our physical education teacher and had a passion for working with the youth. One day while in physical education class, he approached me and told me that I was good in sports. He encouraged me to participate in all the school's activities and try out for the volleyball and track teams. Mr. Schumacher had spoken life over me and ignited the fire within me.

I became even more excited about my abilities and talents, as this was the beginning of my love for education and sports. This would be the trajectory that would set me on my course of exploring and finding my purpose in life. He would be the first of many angels (mentors) who would show up at the right time and right place to guide and provide me with the tools that I needed to navigate and prevail.

As I reflect on my life growing up in the inner city of Cincinnati, the beginning of my journey, love for education, sports and life truly began in the fourth grade. Sports became my outlet early in my life. I was always outside playing either with the boys or competing in various competitions. Mr. Schumacher constantly reminded me how talented and smart I was. He told me that I was a natural-born athlete and would be good in sports. I didn't know then what a natural-born athlete meant, but I sure liked the sound of it.

All the students in the fourth through sixth grade were required to participate in gym. No one had a choice; it was mandatory. I couldn't even imagine why someone would not want to participate in gym. I remember it being fun and exciting. We were required to participate in all the various activities. We climbed the ropes, which I thoroughly enjoyed, flipped on the rings, uneven bars and jumped over the horse like a gymnast. Jumping on the trampoline was optional, but I made it part of my everyday experience. At recess we played kickball, softball, tether ball and raced each other. I enjoyed every moment. I never wanted gym or recess to end. I looked forward to gym every day.

When it came time to fill the sports teams, Mr. Schumacher identified those from gym who he believed could compete and invited them to either tryout or just put them on the team. I made the teams and became even more excited. I was in love with sports and I believe sports loved me.

> **This would be the trajectory that would set me on my course of exploring and finding my purpose in life.**

This newfound gift prepared and started me on my path to a successful career in sports. I realized that sports added volume to my life and opened up a desire to excel in academics. Not only did I embrace sports, but also learning. Going to school was enjoyable. School became the place that allowed me to express myself freely.

I experienced a freedom that was unexplainable. I enjoyed performing and competing every day on the playground and in the classroom or anywhere that allowed me to demonstrate my talents. I loved every moment. The attention that I received was the love and togetherness that I didn't realize that I yearned for. I felt invincible.

I had no fear or doubt in my mind; I knew that I could do anything that I put my mind to. That feeling was confirmed by the many accomplishments and continued encouragement that I received from my angels, especially my math teacher and Mr. Schumacher. The feeling was unbelievable, I felt like an eagle, spreading my wings as I soared!

As I mentioned, I strongly believe that all of us have angels that we can see and angels that are always around protecting us. Some of my angels were visible to me, like Mr. Schumacher and my homeroom teacher. They were always encouraging and guiding me throughout my journey.

With that encouragement, motivation and inspiration, I became a competitor. I was enthused about becoming the best version of myself. Once the teams were formed, it was all competition. The two years that I spent at Rothenberg, we competed against other elementary volleyball teams and at the city's track meet, earning trophies and medals for either winning as a team or individually.

It was truly amazing to see all these schools at one place competing in different events at the city meet. I felt like I was in another world. The people, the events, the competition and all the energy that surrounded me were formidable. I had never seen or experienced anything like that. It was exuberating. By the time I finished fifth grade, I was one of the fastest girls on our track team, best in gym among the boys and girls and top player on the volleyball team, including one of the top academic students amongst the boys and girls. I ran the 50-yard dash, the 100-meter and was the third and sometimes last leg of the relay team. I felt strongly about the possibility of pursuing track through college.

Rosetta was the fastest girl on our track team. Everyone tried and wanted to beat her. She was fast as lightning. She also beat most of the boys who always tried to cheat just to beat her. She and I became the best of friends and often we competed. I don't think I ever won. But it was good having her as a friend and on our team. She was a fierce competitor. Every day during practice she was my target. I'm sure she made me faster.

As I continued to find my identity in sports and dance, education became equally important, if not more important, in my growth and development. My joy and enthusiasm for learning became infectious. I developed a love for math and reading. Just like I was recognized for my athleticism, I became recognized for being smart. My teachers in elementary school took a special interest in my excitement for learning. I was always encouraged to do my work with excellence.

I remember that we were challenged to learn our multiplication tables as quickly as possible. Every day in math class our teacher would test each of us to see who knew their multiplications (times tables). The goal was to see who would make it to the first row and finally be the first one to recite their multiplication factors all the way through 12 x 12, earning a yellow star by your name.

As the challenge became more competitive, I found myself to be the only girl in the lead with the boys. I don't recall if I was the first student to recite all my multiplications through 12 without messing up, but I can assure you that I was in the running. To have my name put up as one of the top girls in math and possibly among the top boys in my class was a moment that I had worked hard to achieve. With additional practice and determination, I made it. I had fulfilled my goal. I was excited to see my name with a yellow star amongst the top of the class.

I also had an interest in joining class organizations. It was something innate in me, as it came naturally. My experiences at Rothenberg Elementary were monumental in providing me with a holistic environment that allowed me to cultivate my natural talents, shape my personality and boost my confidence.

I took on the mindset of believing that I could do anything that I put my mind to. This belief was fueled by the constant support from my family, friends and teachers. This belief ignited the passion within as I continued developing an competitive edge. The rewards of accomplishing my goals and being my best at what I did became the driving force that became my DNA. I became very determined to succeed, no matter what circumstances or challenges lay ahead. I felt invincible. Life was wonderful and I was here to live! Later, I would understand on a deeper level that I came to live and live life more abundantly!

My determination to handle challenges would soon be tested. There was a group of girls at Rothenberg who threatened to jump me after school because they didn't like me. I don't remember what, or if, I had done or said something to them that they didn't like. I was a shy girl and didn't talk much in class. I was new and trying to fit in. From time to time they would pick on me and say negative things about me. I was sincerely scared and I didn't know what I was going to do.

At the end of each school day, a different student would be assigned to lead the class out of the building. It was my day to lead the class which happened to be the day those girls planned to fight me. The only thing that I thought that I could do was to immediately run once I got outside of the building.

To my surprise, as we left the building, they went on about their business. I'm not sure why they changed their minds, but I'm sure my angels had something to do with it. Over time, that same group of girls became my friends. Some of them played volleyball and/or ran track as well. I believe once they got to know me, they discovered that the opinions they had about me were not true.

I wanted to excel at everything that I did. I became fearless. There was no doubt in my mind. I used my athleticism and love for school and sports to cope with the challenges that I experienced growing up in different neighborhoods and six different elementary schools. Moving to different elementary schools just about every grade year required me to quickly adapt. I was able to adjust to each new environment and culture because of my love for school. I was eager to learn; I was like a sponge. Where did all this desire and yearning come from?

Knowing myself on a deeper level, I knew intuitively I was born to succeed. I was always more mature than my peers or friends, even though I was always the youngest one in the group. With my birthday being in the early part of September, it allowed me to start school earlier. In the state of Ohio, any child who turned the age of five by September 30th could start kindergarten. Since my birthday fell on September 25, I was able to start kindergarten. I believe that this was a blessing for me. My mom was busy working to keep food on the table for five children. I feel very confident in saying that staying at home another year would have proved detrimental to my growth.

School was where I came alive; my spirit was free. I was able to express myself without being judged. I remember on at least two occasions when I changed schools, initially, I felt alone. On one occasion, we had to draw a picture for show and tell. As I sat alone, I remember drawing a picture of a bear. When the other children saw my picture, they all wanted me to draw one for them. This made me feel good.

I began to understand that I was gifted and saw how others were attracted to me and wanted to be around me. There was a light inside of me that I believe others could see and feel. I did not recognize until later in life that I was allowing the light of God within me to guide me. I was very in tuned to God's presence. Life hadn't corrupted me yet. The ups and downs of life were foreign to me. I had yet to experience the disappointments that would later happen in my life that caused me to temporarily lose my connection with God, my love for living.

Have you too experienced a disconnection with God? Are you still experiencing the love and joy that surrounded most of us at birth? Have the challenges of life taken you off course? What has been your saving grace? And, how have you moved forward and/or overcome?

Regardless of one's religious beliefs, I believe in a higher power that allows us to exist and we are connected to. This higher power is our intuition, our connection to God. This very power exists within all of us. This power within was very evident earlier in my life. I was very much in touch with this power, the very essence of my soul. Unfortunately, as we move along on this journey, the doubts, uncertainties and negativity that we experience leaves us questioning our very own existence, this higher power.

As I reflect on my life, my connection was driven by the joy and happiness that came from school and sports. This was my reason for living and where I connected with this higher power. I encourage you to take time to reflect, to look back on your life and find what gives you peace, joy and happiness. Your purpose. I believe that you will find it within, as I too have found.

Life for me was simple. We didn't have a lot of fancy or expensive things growing up. We enjoyed the small things. Our mother never allowed us to feel that our lifestyle was any less than many of my friends. As a matter of fact, in the neighborhoods that we lived in, everyone seemed to get along well with each other regardless of our socio-economic backgrounds. Maybe there were a few families who had a little more. We were all in the same community. No one looked down on anyone and we always helped and supported each other.

> It uplifted my soul and even still, music has been my refuge during the good and bad times.

We were a village. Neighbors went out their way to make sure no one was left behind. People genuinely cared for each other.

Playing outside was our life. I'm glad that I grew up without technology being at the forefront of our everyday undertaking. Without being consumed by technology, we were able to use our minds and explore. I believe that these were exciting times for my generation and for me. There were so many activities and events to participate in within our community that kept us engaged and active. The neighborhood recreation centers were essential to our survival. The social programs available in our communities kept us occupied and I believe out of trouble. I remain grateful for those programs.

I'm always reminded how precious time is. Each of us has been given a gift and it's up to us to discover that gift and to realize that everything that we need is within. I do believe that if we don't use it, we can lose it. Many of us continue to look outside of ourselves, searching for answers and solutions to our questions and/or challenges. Sometimes we are still asking, "Why am I here and struggling?" Too many are still relying on stimulation from sources outside of ourselves that only leave us void and have left too many of us chasing our tails. Time is a precious commodity and you can never get it back. It moves with or without us. We must use it wisely.

I was so in touch with my journey, moving and evolving right before my eyes. I'm not sure how or when one discovers the moment when they recognize or awaken to their gift, their purpose in life. I never wanted to lose touch with that knowing/feeling. Nevertheless, as I have continued this journey, I recall losing this knowing from time to time.

I can remember, like it was yesterday, how fascinating it was growing up in the Motown era. The Motown era was very real, it was powerful and the music spoke to my heart. It uplifted my soul and even still, music and dance has been my refuge during the good and bad times. Music is and will always be my first love. Feeling the rhythm and beat is in me. A lot of the songs and dance moves that I learned back then remain with me today.

My soul rejoiced, dancing while the music played invigorated me. I was full of zeal and enthusiasm, the same feeling that I believe we all yearn for as we continue this journey called life. We must find our way back to that which gives us joy and a zest for life.

Participating in all the school musicals and talent shows became the norm for me. It allowed me to express my true desire and passion for music and dance without having to pursue it as a career. I remember our school putting on a musical production that would increase my love for music and my desire to dance. I felt the freedom to express myself through entertaining others. It was invigorating and I was alive. I loved the response that I received performing on stage. It was the same as competing in sports.

Our musical production was so good that our music teacher invited area elementary schools to come to our performance. During the performance, my soul was alive, I was caught up in the Spirit.

As I continued to move from school to school during my elementary years, and my journey was forever changing, I still felt the presence of Spirit. We were always encouraged or required to participate in various extra curriculum activities, the holiday plays, current events and simple playground activities competing against our grade level classes.

One of my favorite, anticipated school activities was the celebration of May Day. It was a custom that celebrates the beginning of summer. We would prepare baskets and put sweets, candy and flowers in them and secretly place them on each other's desk. Then each grade would gather together outside and hold a colored ribbon from the Maypole and dance around, weaving in and under each other as we laced up the pole in celebration of summer.

School provided me the space to express myself fully and unconditionally. I wasn't defined by my race, ethnicity, social or economic background or gender. I was recognized for my gifts and talents despite being a female in an era that was uncommon for girls to be good in both sports and education.

In addition to the sports teams and musical production shows, Rothenberg had a class organization for the fifth and sixth graders. It was interesting that we had student government organizations at the elementary school level. I often wondered if this was unique to the schools in Cincinnati, Ohio. I decided to run for the treasurer of our fifth-grade class organization.

It came natural to me. I didn't give it a second thought when the announcements were made. It felt good to my soul. I was running for a position in office. How excited I was. I immediately started preparing for my campaign. I remember my slogan as if it were yesterday. "Vote for me and I'll set you free, I'll give you money on top of honey." How silly of me. I wanted my slogan to rhyme. It was fun. I was in my element.

My classmates and teachers loved me. They affirmed that I was a natural at speaking and had the right personality for the position. I had a personality that seemed to win people over. Running for this position provided me an opportunity to meet more students.

I enjoyed helping others and seeing them happy. The more students that I met, the more students I could touch. I wanted them to see that they, too, had the ability to achieve their goals and dreams.

It was no coincidence that I ended up at Rothenberg Elementary, the exact place where my journey began. Everything was in alignment for me. It was my destiny and I was ready, open and enthused about life. I loved so much being at Rothenberg that I never wanted to miss a day in school. I woke up eager every day to go to school.

Nothing could stop me from going to school. Not even those girls who wanted to beat me up!

What I realized as I looked back on my beginnings and how I immediately gravitated to a path in sports, education and performing on stage, these were my voice before I found the strength and courage to speak up and defend myself. My angels were always protecting me; and I was in touch with them and conscious of their presence.

One day, my sister, who is nine years older than me, didn't come to pick up my nieces, Alesia and Lisa, at our house after she had gotten off work. They had to stay with us over night. When morning came, my sister still hadn't shown up before my mother had to go to work. At that time, only my younger brother, Alan and I lived with my mother and stepfather. Weeks earlier, my mother kicked my two older brothers out because of their inability to follow her rules. During those days, mothers didn't tolerate their children being disrespectful, especially the older ones who couldn't follow their instructions.

Therefore, my mother informed me that I would have to stay home from school to wait for my sister to pick up my nieces, instead of my younger brother, Alan, since I was the older of the two. I was so upset. I cried and cried and tried to convince my mother to let Alan stay behind instead of me. The thought of me missing school was unimaginable. How could my sister be so thoughtless? Why should I be the one to suffer and stay home and miss school?

Minutes later, after my mom left for work and my younger brother headed off to school, I heard someone knocking on the back window of my room. At first, I was scared and then I heard my oldest brother call my name. I went to the window and he asked if Mom was still at home. I told him she had just left for work. He asked if he could come in and clean up and get something to eat while Mom was at work.

I agreed with the understanding that he would watch our nieces while I went to school. I told him that I would make sure I returned home to relieve him before Mom returned. He agreed. You can't imagine the feeling that I was experiencing. I get to go to school. It was like I hit the jackpot. I was in heaven. I hurried up and got dressed and left before he even thought about changing his mind. I only lived several blocks from school. Off and running I went.

I believe I set a record as I set off to school. I ran so fast that I probably beat the cars that drove down the street. Imagine that! I got to the school and to my surprise I was still on time. Everyone was on the playground and I ran straight to where my friends were and told them what had happened. Again, my angels were making a way for me to get to school because of my unwavering desire. Game on!

I had become very popular at Rothenberg and was known for my enthusiasm and infectious smile. I could not have been in a happier place. Rothenberg had ignited the fire within me and prepared me for another change in schools that would come in Junior High.

> **Life is not about the destination**

Have you ever experienced a moment in your life when you didn't want it to end? One where you felt the Spirit and you were in touch with your soul? I believe these are the moments when we are in alignment with God, the Divine. These are the moments that I experienced writing this book and sharing with you from the depths of my soul about the importance of being in tune with our higher self.

This is where I found my happiness and my purpose for being. Life is not about the destination. Because when one goal is accomplished or one chapter ends, the next goal or chapter begins, it is for me about enjoying the journey.

We are faced everyday with questions that I believe either stimulate or encourage us to move forward. What is my purpose, my reason for being? Am

I living out my soul's purpose? Am I in tune with God's plan for my life? Why am I struggling? How did I get to where I am now? Why is this happening to me? Do I really matter? Better yet, do I truly love myself? Do I need love from others to validate my existence? These were some of the questions that I didn't need to answer when I was cognizant of my connection with my soul.

I believe all of us have a calling and some of us realize it sooner than others. Sometimes I wonder why and how I recognized my joy for life at such an early age. Do you take time to ponder and ask the question, "Why am I here?" Knowing is a powerful place to be. Not only did I know that I was connected to my inner being, the God within me, but I also felt it through my everyday expression as a child growing up in the inner city. Life was wonderful to me. I have always been enthused about living my life to the fullest. As I grew older, living life to the fullest gave me meaning and purpose. It became my cornerstone. I found so much joy and enthusiasm for life that I wanted everyone to feel the same way.

Have you taken time to ask yourself what gives you joy and what resonates with your soul? I believe when we take time out of our busy schedules and spend quality time with ourselves, the answers will come.

Most of us haven't learned how to be with ourselves, spending the quality time with God in prayer and meditation. It seems that we are always looking outside of ourselves, being entertained or searching for validation from others to affirm our existence. I can honestly say that somewhere along the way of my journey I lost my connection with my soul and began to look outside of myself, as so many of us can do. The beautiful thing is that because the foundation had been laid, I have been able to reconnect through prayer and meditation by going within.

I realize I am exercising some self-talk as I am inquiring about life's purpose. As I have shared with you about spending quality time with oneself, I too must heed my own advice. My journey up to now has been a wonderful, yet challenging experience. Finding one's way after realizing that something is missing, or you have lost you way, can leave you asking often, "Why am I here?" What is necessary for me to survive, flourish or strive? Who can I go to for guidance? Am I complete, whole or did I need my mother and father's love to continue to sustain me? My mother was always there. But what about my father?

I hadn't realized that I yearned for my father's love and guidance. I didn't think that growing up without my father affected me until later in my life when I started dating and seeking more personal relationships. I had to rely on my mother's advice and my own intuition. I never got a chance to really know my father. I don't recall him ever living with us. He was always a distant figure. Back then, as far as I was concerned, having a father around really didn't affect me. I was so in tune with God at that time and that was all that really mattered.

The last time that I recall seeing my father, I was eight years old. This may have been the first time I saw or recognized him as my biological father. Unfortunately, it was also the last time. He had come to see us before taking a trip out of town. I remember seeing this tall, very dark skinned, well-dressed, black man. I think he picked me up, because I recall looking into his eyes. I had no recollection of seeing him before.

I then heard my mother say, "The next time we see you, you will be coming home in a box." I did not understand what she meant until almost a year later. My brother and I were told that our father had been killed in New York. He drove cabs in New York and allegedly someone had robbed and killed him. Unfortunately, we did not get a chance to attend his funeral because no one had contacted my mother until weeks after the funeral.

My suspicion is that we, my brother and I, were the outsiders—born out of wedlock to a married man. After speaking with my mother, I am unsure as to what really happened to my father. His life and death remain a mystery to me.

It is one of my goals to get some answers and hopefully bring closure. If I had a chance to meet and be with a person from the past who no longer resides on the earthly plane, it would surely be my father!

As I continued to move forward in my life, several father figures began to appear in my life. Besides my stepfather, their presence would prove to be timely and significant. The advice that I received from them about dating boys and being mentally tough in sports was very instrumental and much needed.

Looking back, I needed my father. Although my mother remarried, our stepfather didn't take on the role as a father figure. He was my mother's husband. He was not a well-educated man and did not have the knowledge of what we needed in a father. He was a provider.

As I moved through elementary and junior high school, the males who took an interest in my talents became more of a father figure to me. These were my coaches and teachers. They seemed to always recognize my gifts and talents. They were very encouraging and took extra time tutoring and giving me pointers about the game of basketball. My coaches and teachers were very tough on me and didn't allow me to give up and make excuses just because I was girl. These lessons and teachings would eventually make me stronger.

I became so good in sports earlier on that when it came to picking teams for various sports and activities, I was either the first girl to be selected or sometimes the first person. Competitiveness became my identity. I always wanted to win. Growing up with three brothers taught me how to protect myself in many ways. They too were always challenging me. Many times, we would go to the playground and play the game of horse to see who would win. As I got better at it, I started beating my brothers and this gave me more confidence in my ability to play and compete with the boys in school and in my neighborhoods.

Chapter 2
MY NEW BEST FRIEND

As I moved along throughout junior high and high school, I got better and better. I developed a true passion for sports. I never wanted to stop playing. This was my life; this was who I had become. Sports became my best friend, my outlet and my ability to express myself without being judged or teased by the neighborhood children. Although, I was very confident in my physical abilities, many times I felt unattractive. I was tall and skinny with long legs. My friends always teased me about my size.

Because I was good at sports, many people called me a tomboy. At that time, it was the norm to call a girl that if she played sports. I would be the only girl outside who wasn't afraid to participate in any of the things that the boys did. I climbed and jumped trees with them, raced and swam with and against them and performed other dare devil activities that girls weren't supposed do. I even wrestled around with them and surprisingly found a kiss planted on my face!

Although I wasn't the prettiest girl in the crowd, I sure enjoyed hanging out with the boys. They liked me because I was one of them. And they were always challenging me to one-on-one in basketball and racing.

My first competition against the boys happened at the local YMCA. I signed up to participate in a one-on-one basketball game and the winner would earn a prize. Honestly, I don't remember what the prize was, nor did I care. I just wanted to compete against the boys. I was the only girl who competed and guess what? I won. Everyone was shocked and surprised that a girl had beat the boys and won the competition. I was ecstatic. My beliefs and confidence in myself grew. It felt good to beat them, because most of the time, they thought they were going to win.

I remember on a few occasions and even now, that the boys and men that I have beat either in basketball or racing have always found an excuse as to why I had beat them. Most would always say, "I let you beat me." Can you imagine how I felt? I had earned every basket and crossed the finish line first.

One day in high school, there was a boy on the boys' basketball team that liked me. He challenged me to a basketball game and I won. He got so mad that he threw the ball at me. Luckily, it missed me. He warned me that if I told anyone that I had beat him, he would deny it and never speak to me again. It would be his word against mine. I wasn't at all intimidated. I couldn't wait to tell everyone. I felt exhilarated and overjoyed. I had just beat one of the boys on the basketball team and now I had bragging rights. I became even more determined to be my best. This was a turning point and lesson for me.

From then on, before I played one-on-one basketball games or races with the boys or men, they would have to assure me that they would play or race me straight up or I wouldn't play or race them. Unfortunately, and even until this day, I have a college friend that I beat fair and square in a game of basketball and a race, but his ego won't allow him to accept defeat by a woman.

All the hard work, dedication and sacrifice that I had made during my earlier years paid off. I was a natural-born athlete. From the first organized team that I played on, my natural abilities allowed me stand out from the crowd. It was exciting.

I was always willing and open to allow the Spirit within me to operate. I now recognize that I was in tune with my higher self, the Divine and was a vessel through which the Holy Spirit expressed itself. The Word says to let your light shine from within so that others may see the glory of God.

My light was bright and I was shining! I felt unconquerable. No one could stop me or tell me otherwise. I could be who I wanted to be. This was my attitude. This confidence became my mindset as I moved through the last year in elementary school and continued my journey to junior high school (now called middle school). I made a promise to never allow myself to forget all the hard work, determination and sacrifices that built my confidence.

Summers as a young child were filled with great memories. As we ran the streets of Cincinnati, from community centers to recreation parks to baseball games, we were always outdoors. Being outside was the way of life for my generation. No one wanted to be in the house. As you could imagine, there wasn't much to do in the house. We only had a TV and a music box to entertain us.

We didn't have all the distractions this generation has and didn't rely on the artificial intelligence of computers, iPods, video games, cell phones, etc., to entertain us or make information readily available. We were able to be creative and develop our critical thinking, the ability to think and reason for ourselves. We were held accountable and responsible for our actions. There was no one or thing to blame.

Many times, we would hold our own neighborhood talent shows, challenging each of us to perform our favorite song or artist. I remember during fifth grade at Rothenberg, our music teacher required the fourth through sixth graders to participate in a musical production that received rave reviews in our community. I can remember it like it was yesterday. We rehearsed a few times a week. I remember the theme. It was based on the Broadway musical production, Hair.

We performed many of the songs recorded by the group, The Fifth Dimension, such as, "Aquarius," "Let the Sunshine In," "Up and Away," and my favorite, "Let it Be," by the Beatles. These songs lifted and inspired my soul. The production also included songs from Tina Turner, such as "Rolling on the River." At that time, I didn't realize how much of an affect these musical productions would have on my life. I was in the movement, feeling the rhythm and beat that I know is a part of my heritage, the pure essence of who I am and where I come from.

The summer following my fifth grade, we moved to another community. Although I was excited that we were moving into our first house, I was very sad that I had to leave Rothenberg. I believe the only way that I was able to adjust was because I had gotten used to moving to different schools.

> **We were held accountable and responsible for our actions**

My experience at the new school was an adjustment academically. I didn't feel the same love and care from the teachers that I had felt at Rothenberg. Nevertheless, I made the adjustment because of the friends that I had made in the community. For some strange reason, everyone was excited about the new family that was moving into the community and Alan and I were able to make friends quickly. Unfortunately, I don't recall if Windsor had sports teams, musical productions or clubs that I could join. I was glad when the school year ended.

That summer before junior high school was very memorable. There was a family of 17 that lived diagonally across from us. Our families became close. They were a sports-orientated family who loved playing sports. We were always hanging out at the schoolyard, which was directly across the street from where we both lived. That probably was one of the only things that I liked about Windsor. When winter came, we didn't have to worry about standing outside waiting for the school buses. All we had to do was literally run across the street and in two minutes we were in school.

Every day during the summer we were outside enjoying our lives. Those were the days of Red Light, Green Light, Mother May I and Hide and Go Seek. We played kickball, four square, hopscotch, basketball and softball.

Softball was one of my favorite sports. Everyone challenged each other to hit the ball over one of the two fences that surrounded the schoolyard. My best friend, Oralee and I were the only girls who consistently hit the ball over the fences. She was from the family of 17.

We were the first two girls to get picked as they formed the teams. Again, because of my athleticism, I was always the first girl to get picked for all the sports and was liked by the boys. They treated me as if I was one of them. Only one or two of them wanted to be more than a friend. Nonetheless, I enjoyed competing with and against them.

I always wanted to outdo them, because most of them didn't accept that girls could play sports at their level. I proved myself. I didn't have any more issues or challenges. I looked forward to playing outside with my friends every day.

There were days when we had to find other things to do. Those were really the best days. We had to learn to entertain ourselves. Jacks, marbles, board games and racing each other became the highlight of the day. We wanted to see who was the best and the fastest.

On raining days, we would find Popsicle sticks, somehow label them and as the water flowed down the streets from the rain, we would challenge each other racing our sticks. On snowy days, we used cardboard boxes and garbage can lids as sleighs because we either couldn't afford them or didn't have them. It really didn't matter. We found ways to improvise.

I always wanted to win at everything I did and participated in. My soul rejoiced as I crossed the finish line first and finished first in all the other games. I believe I was born a winner! Everything that I have been a part of or competed in, I wanted to give my best. I believed at an early age that I needed to win, be first to get recognized for all my hard work. As mentioned earlier, I believed that I came here ready and prepared to do great things. It is my legacy to leave my mark.

I have come to realize that life is what you make it. No one can stop you from being great or fulfilling your purpose and destiny other than you. This strong belief has been sharpened and refined by the encouragement, support and inspiration of my mother and many of my mentors along the way. My commitment to helping everyone achieve their goals and dreams has also always been a part of my journey.

Going to church was a great part of my childhood upbringing. My mother was very involved in church. She sang with a well-known women's group, The Lattimore Sisters of Cincinnati, Ohio, during most of my early childhood. We had to attend Sunday school and were required to sing in the children's choir. Sometimes we had to travel with our mom when the group traveled to other cities to sing. Most of the time, we would be outside playing while they performed.

It was mandatory for all my brothers and sister to attend church if they lived in my mother's home. If they didn't go to church, they would have to stay outside of our house until we returned from church.

I remember, at that time, going to church was an all-day event, from Sunday school to evening services. However, most of the time our mother would allow us to go to the movies after regular service if we behaved ourselves in church. Movies were our outlet from having to stay in church all day, so you can believe that we made sure to be on our best behavior so that we didn't have to stay in church all day and go to the movies instead.

The movie shows were very different from today's movies at the theater.

We got to see two one-hour movies with cartoon shows in between. Some of the movies that were shown during that time targeted our community, depicting racial stereotypes and westerns showing a lot of killing. The most popular movies that we enjoyed were Shaft, Kung Fu with Bruce Lee and movies about black entertainers.

Although movies like Shaft became a part of our culture and were our heroes at that time, they too were very stereotypical. We were inundated with movie star role models who lived in impoverished communities, the ghettos, prone to criminal activities, with black women depicted as single parents living on welfare and/or as prostitutes.

I believe that attending church and learning about God was very instrumental in shaping my beliefs, along with my love for education, sports and music. We sang in the children's choir just about every Sunday. Marching to the beat of the drums and singing from the depths of our hearts, our souls were expressing our love for God.

As a child singing in the choir, we were always recognized and praised by the adults. Parents were proud of their children and the choir directors shouted with joy to see their work come to light by these willing and able little souls. We all dressed up in our white tops, with the girls usually wearing blue skirts and the boys wearing black pants.

We would march down the aisles, moving from side to side and singing all in unison. We were always the highlight of the services. For us, this was the best part of being in church as a youngster as it also meant that we wouldn't have to sit still in church all morning and part of the afternoon.

In addition to singing with the Lattimore Sisters, my mother started pursuing other ministry opportunities. As the group started to travel and sing less, my mother began preaching in small churches around the area. She was ordained and soon pastored her own small church.

We found ourselves in church at least three to four days a week, including all day on Sundays sometimes. We followed my mother around town as she spoke at different churches. This was truly the beginning of my spiritual and religious insight about God.

Most of the time, it was Alan and I who traveled with my mother because we were the youngest of the five and my mother didn't trust leaving us alone with our older siblings. Therefore, we had no choice. Our mother would include us in the process by sometimes having us read Scripture and all of the time, to sing with or without her.

In the world, but not of it! I now realize what Jesus meant. Although my physical body was in this three-dimensional world, my spirit, the essence of my being, was very much connected with the Divine and I was operating at a level far beyond my comprehension.

I now see that is how I was able to withstand the many challenges that I experienced and even those that were unknown to me. For example, there was racism, discrimination against the black race, genocide and the lynching of our people all around me. There was a plight to eradicate and annihilate the black race.

There was very little attention given to the social ills and injustices against the black race and humanity, not to mention, black on black crime. As all these events were taking place, I continued to thrive. I was too young to comprehend the enormity of those issues.

For some divine purpose and reason, I believe that I was protected by my guardian angels because I had a mission to fulfill. We all do. There was a separation of my connection between the physical world and the spirit world. Thus, being in the world, but not of the world. Life for me was flowing with very little concerns or worries. I was happy about my life as I played and ran up and down the streets of Cincinnati, seizing every moment and living life to its fullest. Then tragedy struck and my family's world was turned upside down. We were in the headlines.

Vivid images played out in my mind as it all unfolded. I'm not sure who answered the door, but within minutes the Cincinnati Police charged into our home. They searched for my older brothers and asked questions about a robbery that had taken place the night before. I remember being frightened and terrorized as they entered our home with force.

My mom had to be called home from work. It turned out that my two older brothers had been involved in a robbery at one of the local corner stores. Clearly not thinking, they stashed the stolen goods, beer and wine in the basement of our home. I am certain they were clueless about what could happen and did not even consider the impact it would have on our family. Did they think that no one, not even the police, would trace the stolen goods and/or the perpetrators? The dangers that they could put us all through never crossed their minds. Nevertheless, the situation escalated.

Our house was surrounded by so many police cars you would have thought we had robbed Fort Knox. When my mother arrived to ask what was going on, they immediately handcuffed her and put her into a separate cruiser from my brothers and stepfather, who had been handcuffed minutes before my mom arrived. I recall my mom sharing with us that as the police drove her downtown to be booked, they told her that if she didn't stop talking, they could kill her and it would be justified.

> **Every day during the summer we were outside enjoying our lives.**

As a result of this experience, my second year in junior high would not be a time when I felt the freedom to be myself, as I had come to know prior to this unfortunate and unexpected life-changing event. My mother's life had been threatened and I didn't know how we were going to make it. My mother had been accused of being an accessory to the crime and had to stay in jail for a few days. She and my brothers had also been accused of resisting arrest.

Over the next several months, we spent a lot time in court trying to defend our case. I missed many days in class. Despite trying to make the adjustments and keep my focus, it was hard to maintain my grades and keep up with my homework. My grades dropped and so did my attendance. My love for school was now being challenged and overshadowed by the need to support my mother.

I did manage to sign up and make the volleyball and softball teams, which allowed me to keep some focus during this ordeal. Sports had become an essential part of life and as always, allowed me the freedom to express myself even in the face of adversity. I believe it allowed me to cope with all the stress that my family and I were being put through from all the accusations that one family could defend themselves against from the entire Police Department of Cincinnati.

The trial would last for months, as my mother tirelessly tried to defend her family and now her reputation. How could a well-known woman of God, an ordained minister, not have control of her children? Where was she when this was all happening? Did she not know where her older two sons were?

These and many other questions were being asked and used to discredit my mother's character and her position in the religious community. Nevertheless, we continued to persevere in the face of adversity. My mother was determined to defend her family and hopefully find justice in the wake of this misfortune.

Meanwhile, I was at school trying my best to keep my mind off all the challenges that we were going through. We did get a lot of support from the community. They were always encouraging us to stay strong and praying for us. The interesting thing is, despite the turmoil that was happening, somehow

I managed to withstand the pressure of having to balance missing school due to the court sessions and staying strong for my mother. I'm not sure how I made it through. I can say, that again, I was protected by my guardian angels. They kept me safe. I had a mission to fulfill.

As I ponder and think about the chain of events that led up to this encounter, no one could have told me that I would survive without emotional scars. You see, despite the abuse and suffering that my family and I had to go through as we continued to battle with the Cincinnati Police Department and courts, I remained strong and determined to not allow it to affect me psychologically or physiologically.

I continued to participate in various extracurricular activities to keep my mind off the situation. I was not hiding from the challenges, but I needed a reason, a place to continue expressing myself in the middle of all the chaos that was going on, all of which was literally beyond my control.

I joined the spelling bee contest and did quite well. I was excited. Here again was an opportunity to show the world my talents and gifts. The vibe and energy were high. I needed this experience, because I thrived on people, places and events with high energy. Energy fed my soul. The journey was continuing to unfold.

As a result of the encounter with the police, my mother lost her case. I'm not sure if she wanted to or had enough fight left in her to get the justice that she, and we, deserved. Nevertheless, we had to move again. She decided to give up the house and allow herself and us, to move on and possibly heal from the emotional scars that we had experienced. The move would only involve my mom, Alan and myself. My older brothers remained in jail and once they

> My love for school was now being challenged and overshadowed by the need to support my mother.

were released they found their own place. We moved twice more before I finished high school.

Going to high school was big in my day and my journey getting there was an exciting one. Everyone seemed to take pride in the fact that you were going to high school. It meant that you had grown up and everyone in the neighborhood looked up to those in high school. We were considered the leaders and respected.

There was an assumed responsibility that you were expected to uphold and everyone in the community depended on you to make the right decisions and be an example for the younger children. We were expected to model positive behavior and look out for them. Isn't it strange to know that you have a mission and to know that everything that you do or don't do is a part of your journey?

Chapter 3
THE HALLS OF HIGH SCHOOL

In 1975, I headed off to high school. The structure of the Cincinnati public schools had changed. The junior high schools would add the sixth graders and remove the ninth graders and now be called middle schools. The high schools would now house ninth graders.

As I entered the halls of my high school, Hughes High, "The Spirit of '76" was posted on the walls throughout the building. The senior class had chosen it as their theme. The energy was high and everyone seemed to be in rhythm and flowed with ease. I remember how proud the upperclassmen were and the confidence that they had in themselves. I couldn't wait to become an upperclassman. The ones that I observed were very good leaders and I wanted to be just like them; confident, happy and assured.

I was enthused about the new chapter in my life called high school. I can remember it as if it were just yesterday. My first week of school prepared me and set the stage for an adventurous and promising four-year high school journey at Hughes High School. I transitioned and started my next chapter of playing organized sports at a higher level.

Unbeknownst to me at that time, this would become my ticket out of Cincinnati to fulfill my dreams and goals of becoming a well-known athlete, playing in the Olympics and hopefully, playing professional basketball should it exist. Thirty-four years later, I would return to Cincinnati, Ohio, to be inducted into the Cincinnati Public High School Athletic Association in commemoration of my contributions and achievements that I believed originated from that first momentous week of starting high school.

Every day was an opportunity to become better and I was open. As I moved throughout my freshman year, I was like a sponge. There were so many wonderful and exciting things happening all around me, despite the events taking place in our country. You could feel it in the air. Everyone was moving and grooving. I didn't notice or sense any negative or unusual behavior other than the occasional disagreement or fistfight here and there.

I was in my own world, but I was not unattached from the daily challenges of life. Once again, I was in the world, but not of the world. I felt a sense of peace within me. Nothing was going to stop me from being and doing the things I loved. I was determined! Life was wonderful. Great things were taking place in my life, the world was full of excitement and once again, I felt free. Nothing affected me. I was protected by my angels. I realized that we all have a purpose and a mission to fulfill, no matter what situations or challenges we are facing or experiencing.

Although my freshman year in high school was full of excitement, it was not without the challenges of navigating high school. I was both eager and nervous about how I was going to adjust and fit in. Everyone was moving to and from as if they were on a mission. I soon realized that the mission was getting to classes on time and completing and turning in homework assignments.

> I was enthused about the new chapter in my life called high school.

Handling the everyday humdrum to balance life and school was the goal all along to stay focused and graduate. The first thing that I looked for were ways to find out if they had sports teams for girls and who I needed to contact. I was eager to try out for every sport. I looked forward to continuing my quest and love for sports.

First up, volleyball. I was excited, but nervous about trying out for the volleyball team. I felt high school volleyball would be much harder and more competitive than elementary or junior high. This was the first sport that I played in high school and continued with basketball, softball, then added track and field over the next four years. Playing sports, mixed with academics, would continue to be my stage to express my freedom of being alive while enjoying the spirit of competition.

I tried out and made the varsity team. This was a major accomplishment to make the varsity volleyball team as a freshman. It would serve my spirit well. Practice was hard work, yet fun and exciting. I thoroughly enjoyed the volleyball coach during my freshman year.

The coach knew her stuff and taught us all the fundamentals. The one skill that I remember her teaching the most was how to get under the ball while controlling our fall. This technique would enhance my performance in other sports that I participated in later on. My confidence increased. Over the next four years, I would develop and grow to become of one the best players on the team.

The most interesting and unbelievable thing happened. There were at least seven to eight girls, including myself, who had made the team. We were very competitive and always finished as one of the top teams in the city league. We all continued to play volleyball together over the next four years creating a strong bond of friendship and cohesiveness. Most of us followed each other and played all the other sports of basketball, softball and track and field. Beginning my sophomore year, our high school would go on to dominate girls' sports within the Cincinnati Public High School League with me leading the way.

Next up, basketball. There it was: "Announcement: Hughes High School Girls' Basketball Team holding tryouts for girls interested in playing basketball." Basketball? Remember my best friend, Oralee, from the family of 17? Well, we decided to try out because we didn't want to sit around doing nothing until softball and track season started, both of which followed basketball season. We had grown up together playing basketball and softball with the boys in the neighborhood and were considered the most athletic and talented girls in our neighborhood.

We proudly wore our label of "Tom Boy." We didn't know much about basketball other than what we had learned playing on the playground with the boys in the neighborhood. The boys had taught me to fight and made me a tougher person and competitor. It was all about winning; staying on the court and not being forced to wait for the next available game. It could be a long wait if you lost.

The playground was always full of the neighborhood boys and Oralee and I eagerly awaited our opportunities to prove that we could compete and earn their respect. And prove we did, on many occasions. Sometimes, we would be the first to be picked as the boys formed their teams. We had won them over and carved a name, not only for ourselves, but also for girls.

It felt good that we helped erase the myth that girls couldn't play basketball or be competitive in other male dominated sports. In this era, girls were expected to seek domestic work as defined by society. Cooking, cleaning house and secretarial jobs, amongst other domestic work, were the accepted type of employment for women. It was very stereotypical.

Women athletes before us like Wilma Rudolph, Athena Harris, Ann Myers Billie Jean King and other successful female athletes, were pioneers and trailblazers that overcame the adversities and challenges that female athletes faced in the male dominated sports world. I believe that we were unaware that we also helped raise the benchmark for girls to be recognized for their athleticism like their male counterparts. We would benefit from their fortitude as we stood on their shoulders determined to continue their hard work, sacrifice and legacy.

I was long-legged, thin and awkward, yet strong and confident that I could hold my own. The competitor that I had become increased my thirst for winning. Winning became my goal in everything that I did. This attitude gave me the will power to try out for the team. Oralee and I both made the junior varsity team and would later be moved up to the varsity team toward the end of the season to gain experience and to prepare us to replace the top seniors that would be graduating.

This was the beginning of a great and successful basketball career as a player and coach that would last more than 40 years and it continues to unfold.

My freshman year would be filled with learning and an exciting season, both on and off the court. I learned how to play basketball in an organized setting, while balancing out my class schedule. With school being my haven, while there, I was in my own world. I enjoyed hanging out with my newfound friends, running the halls of Hughes High School and traveling around the city competing against the other high school teams within our league.

My days at school were long because of our practices and games. Many times during the week, I got home late in the evenings, usually after 7:00 PM on practice days and 9:00 PM on game days. I was eager to get up the next day and start all over again. This long and arduous schedule would ultimately prepare me for college.

As I reflect, I can see that my path was being laid out right before my eyes. Every day, I was growing and following my passion, keeping my focus on my dreams and goals of becoming a great and successful basketball player with the hopes of playing in the Olympics. As I moved forward, I worked diligently on achieving my goals. I was still very much in touch with and aware of my soul's purpose. I understood that I was free to express myself and that my life was forever expanding.

During my freshman year, our basketball team was comprised of mostly freshman. The influx of the students that came because of the restructuring of the Cincinnati public school system increased the chances of girls participating in sports and the likelihood of getting some girls that had some skills and/or played sports earlier for either their elementary or middle schools.

Sports were big for the youth in Cincinnati. We had recreation centers, community centers and the Salvation Army Centers that provided board games, arts and crafts activities and organized various sports teams. There were always activities and clubs available in the inner city. As a result, I believe it kept most youth out of trouble and gave us an outlet and a place to grow and stimulate our minds.

The last few games of my freshman year would leave a lasting memorable moment that I will always treasure. I had been moved up to the varsity team, not because of my skills, but because of my hard work and determination. My coach admired my aggressive demeanor on the court and the love that I demonstrated for the game.

I was not going to mess up this opportunity to play on the varsity team. I had approached my coach a few games before the end of the season and asked if I was ready to play varsity. She informed me that when the time came, she would let me know.

Then it happened. The time had come. I found myself playing in the most intense game of our season. This would be the game that secured my place on the varsity team. It was more than I could ever have imagined. I don't remember playing that much in the game.

What I do remember was that it was my first encounter witnessing a fight that broke out between our team and a well-known private school, Princeton High School. Princeton was and still is, known as an elite high school with high academic standards. The fight began when one of my teammates, Geneva, swung at the Princeton player. As I watched from the sidelines, after being instructed by our assistant coaches not to leave the bench, I couldn't help from being a little shocked.

Was this what playing on the varsity team was about? Did I need to be ready to protect myself and prepare myself mentally and physically should this happen to me?

> The competitor that I had become increased my thirst for winning.

The energy in the gym was high. Everyone seemed to get excited and the emotions of the players, coaches, fans, administration and officials were all over the place. Everyone was either trying to get in on the action or stand back and enjoy the moment.

When the situation was brought under control, we finished the game. I'm not sure who won. It really didn't matter to me at that moment. The excitement that I experienced with my first varsity game was far more memorable than winning the game. On the ride back home, that experience became the highlight of our conversation. We laughed and laughed as Geneva recounted the story on how determined she was to get hers in to prove to the Princeton girls that she could handle her own. Attending an elite school never makes you better than someone who does not.

The seniors on our team were always encouraging us to work hard on the court and in the classroom. Two of the standout seniors would go on to play for the University of Cincinnati on a full academic and athletic scholarship. They often planted seeds in our minds that if we continued to be successful as a student athlete that by the time we graduated we too could earn a basketball scholarship to college.

A basketball scholarship? I had never heard of that until they brought it up. This would now become the motivating factor for me. It helped me to realize that my dreams of becoming a great athlete were possible. The season would end and I would return next season as a varsity player. What an accomplishment. I believe it was destined to happen. Everything seemed to line up perfectly. Transformation was taking place right before my eyes.

In the classroom, I adjusted to the academic regimen, balancing both academics and athletics. The teachers and some of my classmates, often complimented me during class. We usually discussed the girls' sports teams and how good we were. This discussion usually followed the morning announcements over the school's intercom with the results of all the games played the day before. The announcements included the top performers and I was usually one of them. As I walked the halls, those who recognized me gave me high fives, congratulated me and encouraged me to keep up the good work.

Honestly, softball was my first love compared to basketball. I grew up playing softball as early as nine years old. This was a popular sport for girls in Cincinnati. We played in elementary school during recess. I played two years in junior high school and we competed against other middle schools. If that were not enough, we would play in the neighborhood after school and on the weekends.

I never got enough of playing softball. Softball was my world. I literally ate, drank and slept softball until I found my love for basketball at the end of my freshman year. The Cincinnati Reds became my preferred professional baseball team. I had developed a love for going to the games because I enjoyed playing softball and watching baseball immensely.

Oralee and I would either put our change together or get money from family and friends and buy tickets to the Reds' games. I believed we attended just about all the home games that our money could afford. We would liken ourselves to the players based on the positions that we played.

Since I mostly played first base and catcher, I always patterned myself after the well-known Reds' first base player, Tony Perez and the famous catcher, Jonny Bench. Oralee played shortstop and second base and would pattern herself after shortstop, Dave Concepcion, and the second baseman, Joe Morgan. They were a great baseball team during my era. I remember when they won the World Series in 1976; it was my freshman year. Our school had warned everyone that if we left school to go downtown to the celebration, we would all be suspended. No one paid them any attention and just about everyone who loved the Reds left school and joined in on the celebration. I don't believe anyone was even reprimanded. We admired the Reds. It was an awesome experience.

The games were always full of excitement. Most of the time we could only afford the upper seats, but we would work our way down to the lower seats after the seventh inning to get a closer glimpse of our heroes. We were also able to earn three sets of tickets if we made the honor roll during any one of the four quarters. You can best believe that this incentive encouraged me to make the honor roll every quarter. And I did.

Over the next few years, we would collect a lot of Reds' souvenirs and memorabilia, such as autographed pictures, posters, bats, baseball caps and baseball cards. The boys in our neighborhood enjoyed trading baseball and football cards with us. In addition to getting the baseball cards at the games, we would also get them out of the Crackerjack box, comic magazines and the ones wrapped in the large bubble gum packages. Those were the days when the small things meant more than the large things. Life seemed all so simple, yet complex.

I had a serious collection that I know would have been worth a lot of money today. Unfortunately, my collections were later destroyed in a flood while I was away during my freshman year in college.

Freshman year was over and school was out for the summer. I was on a mission to improve my basketball skills. Playing on the basketball team and now being a varsity member, I needed to sharpen my skills. I was eager to get on the playground and play with the boys.

Every day I was outside playing basketball at the courts. I learned a lot from the neighborhood boys. They played me tough and didn't cut me any slack. I got knocked down many times, my shot attempts were blocked on different occasions and sometimes I got dunked on. This only made me tougher. I was determined to prove myself and earn my right on the basketball court with the older and stronger high school boys and even sometimes with the college boys who came home for the summer.

I got better and better. I was becoming the person that I was born to be. I was so full of life and purpose. This was my path. I was born to play sports along with my love for education and dance. We would spend countless hours on the playground playing basketball, four-square, hopscotch, tater ball and any other game we could find to play.

We never wanted it to end. We would stay outside all night long if we could. Many times, after we finished playing basketball, we would head right to the pool for a swim and hopefully to cool down. My mother would get so angry with me because my skin would get so dark. Every now and then she would limit my time outside. This bothered me to no end. On those days, I would just sit in my room and play my music.

During the sixties, our music was recorded on vinyl records and albums, unlike today's versions. These records were called 45's and 33's. The 45's played single songs and albums, the 33's, played a lot of songs by the recording artist on both sides of the album. I had a collection of the Motown era music. At that time, it was very inexpensive to purchase the single records (45's). I bought them as often as I could. Most of the time my siblings bought the albums and I often listened to theirs.

While in my room on those days I was required to come in early, I played my records over and over until I learned the words. I often found myself choreographing dance moves to the songs while imagining myself on stage. I would get caught up and forget my troubles and find myself dancing to the rhythm within me.

I felt my connection with God. I felt as if I was in my own world. I was untouchable. No worries, no concerns. I just wanted to be free to express myself in the joy and happiness that had come upon me. At that moment, I felt good. Each day I looked forward to experiencing those feelings as I moved about.

Many of my accomplishments would not have come without the lessons that I learned while traveling with my mother as she ministered and pastored at several churches around the Cincinnati area. My siblings and I were always required to go to church. It was law in our household. However, by the time my younger brother, Alan and I started high school, we were the only ones mandated by my mother's rules. By this time, my older brothers and older sister had left the household and were living on their own.

Most of the time, Alan and I enjoyed traveling and going to church with our mother. In addition to being able to hang out with the other kids at the churches, Mom would always stop to buy us something to eat after church. We really liked that. If we ever wanted to get out of going to church with her, she would remind us that we were going to stop and eat and she knew this would change our minds!

My character was being shaped by the valuable lessons that I was exposed to as I listened intently to my mother preach the Word after being required by her to either read a Scripture and/or sing a song before her message. We were required to learn the books of the Bible and had to practice reciting them either to my mother or at Sunday school and church.

Moving seemed to be the story of my home life, even throughout my college years. Although we were always moving, we never moved outside of the Cincinnati area. All the moves were either back to the communities we once lived in or no more than a ten to fifteen-mile radius.

> Life seemed all so simple, yet complex.

I adjusted to relocating, but I remember telling myself that if or when I got married and had children, I would make it a point to find stability and keep my children in a stable environment and keep them in the same schools through high school. I am glad to say I made sure of this.

So there I was at the end of the summer of my freshman year and starting school in a new school district. This meant that I would have to leave Hughes High and attend the neighborhood school, Taft Senior High School, located in a low-income area referred to as "the projects." Because I had become a standout athlete, my basketball coach got the principal at Hughes High to request a special transfer for me to remain at Hughes as opposed to having to attend the neighborhood school. I was so happy! I had heard negative things about the neighborhood school and I didn't want to leave all my friends and start over with the new school, teachers and coaches. Unfortunately, we could not get a special transfer for my brother, Alan, since he was just starting high school.

As I look, back, I wish I had insisted that they make an exception for him as well. Taft would not prove to be the best path for him. He remained in constant trouble, getting suspended regularly. My brother was a very kind and loving person, but did not back down from anyone. His temper usually got the best of him. I loved and missed him dearly.

My sophomore year would set the trajectory for being recognized and honored for all the hard work, dedication and sacrifices that I had made during the summer months on the playgrounds, at the recreation centers, clubs and the streets of Cincinnati after my freshman year. Although I had dreams and aspirations of doing great things with my life, I didn't expect for it to happen as quickly as it did.

By the end of my sophomore year, I was starting to attract the attention of the city and state newspapers and other local papers as a standout girls' basketball player. This was the beginning of many articles to follow in many of the Cincinnati newspapers about this young black girl climbing her way to the top.

From that point on, I was their star, leading the city league in scoring and rebounding. I had grown a lot since my freshman year. I had been known for being an aggressive defender and got called for fouling a lot. As a sophomore, although I played with more control, because of my aggressiveness and love for the game, I still found myself on the bench more often than in the game.

I was thirsty and hungry for the ball. I knew that if I got the ball from my opponents, I was more than capable of putting it in the basket. I had learned from playing with the boys that stealing the ball from your opponent gave you an opportunity to score and scoring was the highlight of the game.

The lessons that I had learned and earned on the playground playing with the boys had paid off. My basketball coach was impressed with how much better I had become in such a short period of time. This growth seemed to be the same for most of my teammates. As the season progressed, we were beginning to earn a name for ourselves as one of the top and best girls' basketball team in Cincinnati and the surrounding cities, like Dayton and Columbus. We had also carved out a niche in volleyball as well. I was caught up in the energy and excitement of competing. I looked forward to that feeling every time I got on the court or the field—the feeling that my team and I were unstoppable.

Great things were unfolding for my team and me. My teammates and I started to hang out together more often, as most of us continued playing other sports together. At school, we started to become popular and began earning the respect of our peers. We were in rhythm and everything around us was beginning to unfold as if it was divine intervention. We were not, however, without the challenges teams experience as each one is trying to find their role and fit in.

As I began to get most of the attention from the media, some of my teammates began to show signs of jealousy and began to say negative things about me. At first, I was devastated. How could my close friends, who I treated as sisters, turn against me? Initially, I started to doubt myself and decided to play below my abilities, hoping that they would stop talking about me and stop spreading rumors about things that were not true. I sought comfort from my mother and my favorite geometry teacher, Mrs. Gayle. They both encouraged me to keep my head up and try not to let the negativity get me down. They reminded me of how strong I was and that I should keep the faith. Everything was going to be ok.

I took their advice and somehow managed to get through it, although the jealousy and talking behind my back would continue throughout my high school career. I found that these obstacles only made me stronger and more determined to excel. I believe that because of my faith and the support I received from my mother, close family members, teachers who admired me and a couple of friends, I made it through and overcame a lot of different adversities.

In addition to this support, I was able to lean on my strong relationship with God that I had developed during my childhood upbringing in church. We were always encouraged to pray. Prayer and the Scriptures that I had learned kept me going and kept me grounded. I always felt connected to God and I knew my angels were always there to protect me. My strong faith and belief in God became the foundation that helped me to move forward in the face of adversity. I developed an attitude that I would not let anyone or anything stop me from achieving my dreams. I became unstoppable.

I came to realize that not everyone was a friend and that I needed to be mindful of those I kept close to me. Many people had their own motives and often didn't want to see me succeed. At that time, I couldn't understand why people would try to hurt the people that they called friends. It was not in my nature. I always wanted to help others in any way that I could. I wanted everyone to succeed. So, for me, it was hard trying to understand why and how people could be so malicious or inconsiderate.

Aren't we all here to help each other? I believe that we were all born with gifts and talents and everyone must find what theirs is and not be envious of other's gifts and talents. I believe we all have within us the power to be great. That revelation happens at different times for each of us. However, those who take the time to seek it and spend time working on themselves, eventually find it. I found it.

My passion for education and sports allowed me to express my God-given talents while helping others along the way. I wanted my commitment of being the highest version of myself to be an example for others to know that they too were capable of doing the same.

The summer after my sophomore year would prove to be even greater than the one before. It started with my coach putting our team in a summer AAU weekend event. This was the first time that I had heard of AAU, the Athletic Association Union. It's an organization that sets up basketball showcases and tournaments for girls ages 9–18 to demonstrate their talents and skills against other teams with the goal of winning their respected age group.

It was a wonderful and eye-opening experience. I couldn't believe my eyes. There were so many girls at the event and games were being played simultaneously on the same floor. I was nervous and questioned whether I could compete with them.

Our coach expressed to us that she wanted us to get the experience of playing against other teams outside of Cincinnati, mostly white girls, so that we could learn their style of play and how best to compete against them. She wanted us to gain experience and be prepared for our next season should we advance to the regional and state championship tournaments.

I really don't recall how I played. I do remember injuring my finger and I had to sit out a game or two. Usually at these events, teams could play as many as two to three games per day and possibly a total of six to seven games over two days depending on how many games they had won in their bracket. All I remember is the experience. I had been introduced to the world of basketball on the outside and I was ready!

As usual, I found myself on the basketball court in many of our neighborhoods playing now with the older boys and sometimes against college male players. I played them every chance that I could get. I was in love with basketball and it was in love with me. Basketball became my main sport by the time I graduated from high school. It was my ticket out of Cincinnati. I would pursue my dreams of playing basketball through the professional level wherever possible.

During the times when I was not on the court, I was hanging out with my friends in the neighborhood until I started the Upward Bound program at the University of Cincinnati. I was excited about being accepted into the University of Cincinnati's Upward Bound Program, a college preparatory program for inner-city high school students who had expressed an interest in attending college after high school.

During the six-week program, we resided in the dorms on campus during the weekdays and returned home during the weekends. It was a great experience. During the week, we were enrolled in college-ready courses and engaged in extracurricular activities during the later afternoons.

We were introduced to all types of sports, including tennis, which I thoroughly enjoyed, along with golf and of course, basketball. They put us on a daily schedule that mirrored that of a typical college student. It was a great opportunity to be exposed to the college life. We were required to take courses, such as mathematics, laboratory sciences, composition, literature and foreign languages. We were expected to complete all assignments and to successfully pass all of our classes.

In addition to academics, Upward Bound provided tutoring, counseling, mentoring, cultural enrichment, work-study programs, education and counseling services as needed. I recall having to meet with the counselors at the end of the program to complete an assessment and discuss my future plans. We were required to project our plans and goals for the next 5-10 years of our lives. The first time I did it, it was challenging. I attended the Upward Bound program each summer up through graduation and planning became more doable.

The experiences of attending Upward Bound, working different summer jobs and the knowledge that I received from many of my teachers as they shared many valuable lessons about future preparation, helped me to figure out the direction and the path that I planned to take. By the time I finished high school, Upward Bound had prepared me for college.

As my junior year unfolded, my outlook on life was changing. I was being transformed. I realized how passionate I was about helping to tear down the walls of discrimination and the racism that I had been exposed to. Although I remained committed to sports, my desire to become more educated would now become my top priority. I began to hear stories about how colleges and universities were using black athletes for their talents and gifts and that most of them were not receiving the education afforded to them, even though they were on a full athletic scholarship. And the majority of them did not graduate from those institutions. That was not going to be me!

I decided to get more involved in various clubs and participate in student government to use my voice along with other black students whose mission was to help assure that we were being treated equally and received the same education as the white students. I began to take on a personal mission to make sure that I was not going to be known just for my athletic abilities.

One of my goals was to be known as a student-athlete which could potentially erase some of the negative stereotypes that most black athletes were just "jocks" and uneducated. I often encouraged my teammates to do the same. I wanted everyone, not just athletes and especially the black students, to take their education seriously. I wanted them to value the opportunity to learn. Unfortunately, this opportunity was denied to our parents, grandparents, great grandparents, great-great grandparents and all our ancestors. I often quote Arthur Fletcher who said, "A mind is a terrible thing to waste," and I was not going to waste mine.

> **Many people had their own motives and often didn't want to see me succeed**

The appearance of Jesse Jackson at our school would solidify my mission. The auditorium was packed. Everyone was excited to see and meet him. The energy was high and you could feel the positive vibes in the room. His speech was electrifying! Although I knew he was speaking to all of us, I felt as if he had heard my cry and was speaking directly to me.

Mr. Jackson encouraged all of us to accept the mantra, "I AM SOMEBODY," and to repeat it every chance we got. He challenged us to take our education seriously, to read as many books as we could, spend a lot of time in the library, make sure we do our homework and turn it in on time and to pass our classes. He taught us that although black people were looked down on and often treated inhumanely, we are somebody.

That day, Mr. Jackson had asked who in the crowd was the captain of the girls' basketball team? He had heard about the success that we were experiencing on the court. At first, I was nervous, but then I raised my hand and told him my name and that I was one of the team captains. He spoke directly to me. I was in awe. All I can remember is that he challenged me to be a strong leader and make sure that we all went to class and got good grades so that we could go to college.

He reiterated his passion for helping young black children. He too, like me, wanted all of us to succeed and had us repeat, "I AM SOMEBODY," until we all felt it in our hearts. This mantra got me up-and-running and confirmed for me that I was truly here for a reason. There was no doubt in my mind that I was born to help empower others. Sports became the vehicle that has allowed me to show others that they could fulfill their dreams. Regardless of their adversities or the color of their skin, ethnicity, gender or race, they could succeed. I believe we are expressions of the Divine and that the Spirit speaks to us all in many ways. Each of us has our own mission. I AM SOMEBODY. AND YES, YOU ARE TOO!

From that point on, if you wanted to find me between and after practices, you would find me in the library. I was hungry and wanted to increase my knowledge. I wanted to excel in all my classes. I began reading more at home, regardless of how late I got home. I recognized that the library had always been a part of my life. Looking back, I spent a lot of time at the neighborhood libraries during the summers of my childhood life. We found the library to be a good place to hang out, especially when it was hot outside.

A group of us would walk downtown to the main branch because they normally provided the kids with snacks. While at the library, we would put on the headphones and either listen to the stories or music. We participated in all the on-hands activities, arts and crafts and live events. Sometimes the librarians were surprised to see the black children at the library and how well we behaved.

The library was also a place where I was free to dream and use my imagination. Many of the books that we read or listened to were the classic fairy tale stories, as well as those of the lives of famous Black Americans (African Americans). Cinderella was my favorite story and I always likened my life to this fairy tale. As the story goes, she would sit in the corner of the room where she was often locked away by her stepmother, who was jealous of her beauty. Cinderella would often sing, "In my own little corner, in my own little chair, I could be whatever I want to be." Many times, I felt alone in my own space and would often sing that verse to uplift me and remind myself that I could be whatever I wanted to be.

I was and still am, a dreamer. I've always looked for my dreams to come true. And they have! And prayerfully, they will continue. Those lyrics still resonate in my mind and have become one of my mantras. We all have dreams and should never stop dreaming. That's what life is all about! I am a dreamer. I believe God put dreams in our hearts and we were assured that God would give us the desires of our hearts, our dreams!

Chapter 4
DESTINED TO MAKE A DIFFERENCE

Back to the library in high school! There were so many books to read on various subjects. I was amazed. I was attracted to the books on famous Black Americans. I wanted to learn more about black history and the plight of black people and their journey.

As I began to read through some of the popular black magazines like Jet, Ebony and Essence, I had no idea I was in for such a rude awakening. Even though I had heard about black on black crime, I didn't know the magnitude of the impact it would have on my community and me. I was shocked to read that within my own community there were so many senseless killings. Years later in 1990, I would unfortunately experience firsthand the senseless killing of my younger brother, my beloved Alan.

I was compelled to no longer sit on the sidelines and witness heinous crimes, one right after the other. Losing my brother, having a tragedy hit so close to home, ignited a passion in me. At first I was angry, but my anger soon dissipated into grief and mourning for not only the loss of my brother, but for my city.

As I continued to read these types of stories, I couldn't fathom how heartless and cold people could be that they would kill each other for no apparent justifiable reason. It was disheartening that blacks were being killed by white Americans and having to persevere against racism and discrimination. These atrocities are still all too common today. Sometimes, I wonder if these senseless acts will ever end.

Nevertheless, I kept my focus. Somewhere in the back of my mind, I too, like Dr. King, dreamt of a world where everyone would treat each by the content of their character and not the color of their skin and ultimately treat each other with love. I wondered how so many young blacks survived and thrived in neighborhoods riddled with poverty and crime. I thought it would be exciting to play sports with girls who had made it out of those types of neighborhoods. To my surprise, this thought would come true. I would later have the opportunity to play with and against many of those girls in college.

I came to realize that my thoughts were powerful and to be more intentional and mindful of what I thought, said or wished. I'm reminded that sometimes you must be careful of what you ask for because you just might get it. This thought reminds me of one of my many quotes, "If you say you can, you can. If you say you can't, you can't. Either way, you're right." Why not use the positive instead of the negative?

I continued to surge forward with all this newfound information, destined to make a difference. I didn't want to be a statistic: high school dropout, teenage pregnancy, incarcerated or even possibly subject of a senseless killing. I wanted to be known for using my talents and gifts to help others and make a difference in my community.

There were so many stereotypes, myths and racist undertones that I had to face and overcome despite my academic and athletic success. I was determined to help break down these attacks against my character and those of other black students who were working hard every day to achieve their goals and dreams in the pursuit of making it out of the projects, ghettos and other low-income neighborhoods and communities. I, too, had lived in those communities throughout my upbringing.

My junior year would continue to flourish. Great things were happening as our girls' sports teams (volleyball, basketball, softball and track and field) continued to excel. We were making a name for ourselves and I was at the helm. Was I becoming a leader or was the leader in me emerging?

As one of the team captains for each sport that I played, I was the more vocal one. I became the spokesperson who courageously spoke out and stood up for my teams. No longer would I allow us to be treated unfairly, as a student or student-athlete, without speaking up. I had finally found my voice again. I had finally overcome the negative encounter that caused me to stop speaking up for myself when my third grade teacher struck me for no apparent reason. This was a pivotal point in my life. I felt that my life had new meaning and purpose as I took on the mission to help others along the way of my journey.

A TEAM EFFORT

Plan it out...

My junior year would prove to be more than I had expected. The teachers and administrators began attending and supporting our girls' basketball teams at the games. We were the talk of the school, our neighborhoods and the city. Everyone came to know the Hughes Big Red Girls' Basketball Team and that #31, Barvenia Wooten, was their star. By mid-season, with a perfect record of 15–0, we took over the number one spot under the United Press International Ohio Class AAA Girls High School Basketball ranking.

We would continue to dominate the league until we lost in the district championship. The next day after the district championship game, some of my teachers would spend most of the class time talking about the game and how proud they were of our team. Some of us would egg them on as they talked about the game to avoid having to do classwork. I'm sure most of them knew our intentions, but played along with us.

> **I'm reminded that sometimes you must be careful of what you ask for because you just might get it.**

I have very fond memories of our bus rides to and from games. We were a fun bunch and enjoyed being around each other, which helped because we were always winning! We would sing chants on the way there and back, regardless if we had won or lost. Which didn't happen often. We would sing chants like, "We Are The Big Reds, The Mighty, Mighty Big Reds, Every Where We Go People Want To Know Who We Are and We Tell Them, We Are The Big Reds, The Mighty, Mighty Big Reds!"

We would go around to each player and that player would have to lead us in a chant, so by the time we got to the game, we were fired up and ready to play. Our coach didn't have to do a lot to motivate us. We were good at motivating and inspiring each other. It seemed to come naturally. We were so full of energy and love for the game.

We developed a bond that would stand the tests of adversity that we would experience from time to time, whether it was a disagreement among teammates, a teammate being disciplined or challenges that every team experiences, sometimes beyond their control. We couldn't wait for the pep rallies that the school held for all our home games and some of the away games, depending on whom we played and how far we had to travel.

Our band was excellent. They took pride in their work and always played at our pep rallies. Most of us would join in and dance with the majorettes and the cheerleaders during their performances. They always welcomed us; we had a mutual respect. Our band leader was very committed and involved. He always supported us and couldn't wait to see if we had won when we came to school the next day after playing an away game. All the students respected and admired him.

Our practices were always held right after school, usually around 3:30 or 4:00 PM. They were at least two hours and could go longer when we needed extra time to prepare for our tough opponents. We worked a lot on our defensive press, which became our signature and success to winning a lot of tough games. Although we were a nice group of girls, we were mentally tough. Many of our practices were against the practice team comprised of the boys who hadn't made the boys basketball team. Most of them were good. They challenged us and never let up on us. They helped make us physically strong as well, blocking our shots, knocking us to the floor (not intentionally), blocking us out, forcing us to fight through the contact and all the while teaching and encouraging us.

This was uncommon and uncharacteristic, but it worked and paid off for us. They supported us at all our games. They were our biggest fans. We had our own following. Because I had often played against the boys in my neighborhood, playing against them only helped me more. I learned to play a more physical and mental game.

So, when it came to playing against the girls, most were no real challenge to me. I was able to transfer the physicality and skills that I had learned playing with and against the boys. I developed a baseline jump shot because I had to learn to create space to keep the boys from blocking my shots. Many of the articles in the paper always made mention that I was one of the best baseline shooters in the city. I credit the boys for helping me develop this skill.

At that time, we didn't have auxiliary buses for sports and had to carpool, ride the city bus or sometimes the coaches would even give us a ride home. From my sophomore to senior years, the city of Cincinnati recorded 1976–78 as the coldest years in the history of Ohio. The ice stayed on the ground for months and the Ohio River froze in January 1976, packing up to 8–12 inches thick of ice. Can you imagine a river as massive as the Ohio River freezing? Unbelievable.

That meant that we would have to weather the ice, snow and cold for a long period of time. I never looked forward to having to either catch the bus home or walk because it was so cold. I would have to put on several layers of clothing and make sure my hands and head were covered. It would be so cold, with temperatures well below freezing and sometimes in the single digits. By the time I got home, it would take a while before I thawed. This was the way of life in Cincinnati. The news would jokingly make comments that they thought we were going into an ice age. At the time, I thought we would too. It wasn't a joke at all when it came to enduring the extreme cold weather. What's interesting was that no matter how cold it could get, we still had to be at school and on time.

We had true winters and on any given day, we could get large amounts of snow. The one time I recall schools closing was during my junior year was when the forecast predicted that we could get over 20 inches of snow. Mind you, the snow had already begun falling earlier that morning. The announcement came over the PA system that the schools were closing and everyone would be sent home before it got worse. I knew the city buses would be packed.

So, I hurried up to catch one as quickly as I could to avoid having to wait for the next bus. I knew it would be a rush and everyone was trying to get home.

As I took my seat on the crowded bus, everyone was talking about the snow. And then, the funniest thing happened. As a few boys got on the bus at the next stop, one of the boys said to an elderly woman, "Excuse me little old lady with the fur hat," to which she surprisingly replied, "Excuse me little old boy with the fur cap." Everyone, including the bus driver, laughed for a long time. No one had expected her to respond. The bus ride home that day will always be a fond memory. Even as I am writing this, I am laughing.

Life has a way of letting you see that there are just as many good times and memories as compared to the moments that you don't want to remember.

The bad doesn't last long if we can refocus and reflect on the positive experiences. It doesn't matter what those circumstances or situations may be. We have all been given the free will to choose how we respond. The psychology 90/10 rule, which I honestly believe and have applied to my life, says that we control 90% of how we react to things and events and the other 10% is beyond our control.

I continued to make headlines. "March 25, 1978, Junior, Barvenia Wooten, joins Cincinnati Enquirer Newspaper All-City Girls Basketball First Team." The articles and attention continued as the season ended. We had another great year but would somehow lose to one of the top girls' catholic teams in Cincinnati, Mother of Mercy, at the district championship.

They were a tough team and we usually struggled in breaking their press. We joked a lot about their name because for the first three years, they had no "mercy on us." The tides would turn in our favor in my senior year. By now I was starting to draw interest from some of the area universities and colleges.

I was a bit puzzled, however, that I hadn't drawn more interest from colleges from other states given my notoriety. I met with my head coach to find out why. I don't remember exactly what she said, but it didn't make sense to me. The only university that she talked about was the University of Cincinnati (UC). For some strange reason, it seemed as if everyone, my coaches, administrators and counselor, were pushing me toward UC. I wanted to explore the world, spread my wings and pursue my dreams. My goal was to leave Cincinnati as soon as I could; I had no plans to stay home and attend college locally.

During my freshman year, there were a few seniors who had earned scholarships to play at UC. I had been in UC's Upward Bound program for the last two years and did not enjoy the culture outside of the program throughout the campus. I wasn't sure I belonged at a predominately white institution. I had developed a need to help my own culture and wanted to pursue a historical black college or university. There was too much racism and discrimination that I saw and experienced. I realized that it existed all around Cincinnati. I didn't want any part of it if I could choose. It was enough dealing with it in school, even though I was a standout student-athlete.

I believed I received preferential treatment because of my athleticism from some of the teachers and administrators. However, I liked the thought of being recruited by a large university. I told my coach this and she asked me to give her a list of schools and she would contact them and send them my information. I was satisfied until I later discovered that she didn't send my information out until late in my senior year. I was disappointed because I truly felt that she only tried to get me to go to UC.

Softball season came around again. I truly believe that it was no mistake that this group of girls came together at the right time and the right place and that it was divinely inspired. We had built a girls' sports dynasty at Hughes High School and I was excited to be in it. I attributed coming together in this moment as a testament to the grassroots movement that was taking place as black people began to feel good in their skin.

We took pride in ourselves and was motivated, and inspired by the Motown era music artists' songs, like James Brown's, "Say it Loud, I'm Black and I'm Proud," The Temptations, Spinners, Diana Ross & the Supremes and the powerful voice of Aretha Franklin's, "Respect," just to name a few. We danced and moved to the beat and rhythm of these songs. They taught of many valuable lessons and provided us with the motivation that gave us the strength and the power to persevere in the face of adversity. These were life-long lessons that would shape and mold our character.

Another summer and the hard work and determination continued. I was back in Upward Bound and working at my summer job. I was fortunate to work for another angel, a mentor, Dr. Calvin Smith, who was the director of African American Studies at the University of Cincinnati at that time. Dr. Smith had been trying to get in touch with me for quite some time. Initially, I did not want to return his call because I thought that he too was a part of the plan to get me to come to UC. I also initially thought he was white.

Not that I didn't want to deal with him, but I felt that as a white man, he wouldn't have my best interest at heart. I had come to see that our community was not afforded the same opportunities as our white counterparts. I finally decided to call him because I had found out that his daughter played basketball at one of the city teams and that he was black and head of the African American Studies Department. As result, I felt more compelled to call him hoping that as a black professional working at a PWI, he would have my best interest at heart.

My call to him was pleasant and we scheduled to meet a few weeks after losing in the semi-finals of the 1979 Ohio Girls AAA State Basketball tournament. Little did I know, the way I would come to understand the challenges of being black in America during the '70s, would forever change me. After my meeting with Dr. Smith, my view of the world was greatly impacted in a way that I had never experienced or been exposed to before. The information and knowledge that he shared we me was mind blowing!

My senior year started as well as the final chapter of my high school years. The Hughes Big Reds girls' sports teams were the teams to beat in volleyball, basketball and softball. We had come to dominate in all those sports since the beginning of my sophomore year. First up! Our volleyball team captured the 1979 Cincinnati Public High School League title. Volleyball season had become just as enjoyable as basketball.

This victory would not come without some adversity among fellow teammates. As we were becoming more popular and I was getting most of the attention, jealousy and envy would once again rear its ugly head. One teammate had started to build a strong relationship with the head volleyball coach off the court. I noticed that the coach would often give her and some of the other girls a ride home from practices and sometimes after games. From time to time, I would hear them making little comments about me and for reasons beyond me, they started to distance themselves.

At practices, I noticed that the coach complimented her often, more than she did my other teammates and me. At first it really didn't bother me. This coach had taken over the volleyball team during my junior year. I had been a starter on the volleyball team since my sophomore year. Late in the season, during one of our games, she didn't start me and I believed I didn't get to play much. This was strange and unusual to me.

I hadn't missed any practices, I was not injured or hurt, I didn't talk back to the coaches, what could it be? After the games, I asked the coach why I didn't start. She couldn't really explain. Her quick answer was that she wanted to try a new line up. I was not satisfied with her answer. I felt she purposefully did not start me because she wanted the other player to get the attention and less attention for me. I was really upset. Why would she do this to me? I hadn't done anything wrong and there was no honest reason for not starting me.

When I got home, I remember sharing this situation with my mother because I felt hurt and didn't know how to deal with my emotions. This was my first experience of being treated unfairly on an organized team. I was confused about it. This experience urged me to use my voice once again and speak up for myself. It was a valuable lesson that I had learned all too well from my third-grade experience and the encouragement that I received from the Reverend Jesse Jackson's "I AM SOMEBODY" mantra.

> I wanted to explore the world, spread my wings and pursue my dreams. My goal was to leave Cincinnati as soon as I could; I had no plans to stay home and attend college locally.

The next day before practice, I went into the office that both the basketball and volleyball coaches shared. I was pretty upset and unsure as to how I was going to share my discontentment. The moments prior to approaching them, I had even been considering transferring to another school. I was glad that both coaches were in the office when I walked in because it was important to me that they both knew how I felt about being treated unfairly like the volleyball coach had done.

I shared how I felt and what I believed was the real reason for the volleyball coach taking me out of the starting line after three years of being a top performer on the team. I asked for the reason behind the sudden, last minute change to the lineup, without any true reason and without at least letting me know of the change before the start of the game.

At that point, I was reliving the emotions that I felt at the time of the incident. I shared with them that no matter how hard they tried to discourage me or how vindictive they behaved, I believed in myself and my abilities; and nothing was going to stop or hinder me from achieving greatness.

I began speaking from a place of assurance and I felt the spirit within me rise, giving me the confidence to speak my truth. I reminded them that, "I AM SOMEBODY," and one day I was going to achieve more than they could ever imagine. I said that I was aware that Hughes High was not a top academic school and that they didn't care about the education and well-being of the black students.

I mentioned that I had considered transferring to Walnut Hills High School. It was one of the elite academic public high schools in Cincinnati at that time and had sustained its reputation over the years. Some of my friends from Walnut Hills who were also student-athletes shared that Walnut Hills did care about the well-being of their students and their goal was to prepare them for college.

My basketball coach had the audacity to tell me that I was not smart enough to go to that school and that I would not succeed. Imagine that. This is the same coach who had spoken highly of my athleticism, applauded me for my prowess on the court, recognized me for performing on the court and now, was telling me that I was not smart enough. I was offended. Now, I was really on fire. I recall taking a breath as I looked at both white coaches before I spoke.

"IT'S ACADEMIC" TEAM

Sitting between two top school athletes (Wooten and Miller), Captain Sanders spearheaded a victory over Taft and almost overtook Glen Este as well. "James' three years of experience paid off," declared advisor W. Bacon.

Then, out of nowhere, came this booming loud voice. "I AM SOMEBODY. Remember, I am one of the top girls' basketball players in the city and you are only trying to stop me from transferring because it would hurt you and the program more than me. You only care about yourself and you would do anything to block my transfer."

I'm sure I said some other unkind words. But who was she to tell me what I was or was not capable of doing or becoming? I don't recall their response, nor did it matter! From that day forward, I was back in the starting line, performing even better. As mentioned earlier, we would go on to win first place in the city league. I truly believe that I could have also earned a scholarship to play volleyball in college, but basketball had become my love.

Next up! It was basketball season and Cincinnati's Hughes Big Red Girls Basketball was on top and the team to beat, along with its top player, Barvenia Wooten, leading the team and league in scoring. The accolades that we received from the press for our performance were becoming the norm. I was considered the top girls basketball player, not only in the City of Cincinnati, but the State of Ohio. My notoriety was spreading fast.

Throughout the basketball season, my team and I were the headline stories, not just for basketball, but also for girls in sports. The press seemed to be our ally. They enjoyed writing about my team and me. The Cincinnati Enquirer wrote, "Hughes High School Basketball Player, Barvenia Wooten, No longer an Ax." The reporters had come to interview me. My coach explained to them that I had learned to control my fouling and that I no longer fouled (hacked) my opponents.

HUGHES BASKETBALL star Barvenia Wooten shows teammates in left photo why she averages over 20 points per game, then takes a break from practice, above.

Photos For Enquirer
BY ALAN HOWELL

Hughes' Barvenia Wooten An 'Axe-Woman' No Longer

I was an aggressive player and understood that if I could somehow steal the ball, then I could run the court and score. The excitement and enthusiasm that came from scoring the ball was exuberating for me. When I scored, I drew energy from the crowd as they cheered me on. To enjoy that feeling that I got from scoring and to help my team win, I had to make an adjustment. I learned how to control my aggressiveness and not get in foul trouble. Getting in foul trouble put me on the bench and limited my time on the court. This recognition soon became my motivation for staying on the court and allowed me to become an effective player and a challenge for my opponents.

Even the occasional boyfriends that came along were no match or distraction. I was focused and determined to stay true to my dreams and stay committed to be my best with the dream of earning a scholarship to play college basketball. And soon that dream came true.

It's interesting to see that dreams can and do come true. I feel very confident in saying that and it is why I have continued to believe in my dreams. Mine have manifested and I know beyond a shadow of doubt they will continue to unfold. Another one of my favorite quotes that has become a mantra is, "Believe you can and you will." One of my favorite Scriptures says if you have faith the size of a mustard seed, you can move mountains. This belief is rooted deep down in my soul.

The articles kept coming. Wooten continued to make the headlines. I was excited and eagerly looked forward to picking up the city newspapers after games in anticipation of collecting all the articles for my scrapbook. I planned on using those articles as motivation to better my game. Basketball and I became inseparable. Everywhere I went I had my basketball with me. I lived for practices and couldn't wait for the games. With a 22–0 record, we headed to the district playoffs. "Wooten Guides Hughes Girls Past Mother of Mercy."

It was a victory long overdue. Mercy had been our Achilles heel since my freshman year. In my junior year, they came back to beat us from being 16 points behind to capture the district title. Not this time. This time it would be different. We won. This time would be the game that counted. "Tied 78–78, after two overtimes, Barvenia Wooten settled matters with a shot from the side with 23 seconds left and final free throw with three seconds remaining," wrote the Cincinnati Enquirer.

Although this is a distant memory and I knew that we won the game, I didn't realize how we won the game until I read the article as I was writing this book. To my surprise, there I was again, caught up in the moment, playing the game that I love with passion and vigor. At that moment, it was all about winning the game for an opportunity to play in the state tournament.

That was a goal that our team had set sights on since losing in the district championship the year before. It didn't matter who got the credit; it was a team effort. This group of girls, who had started the journey together three years ago, would defy the odds and successfully set the mark for teams to follow long after we all left.

As I looked back and reflected on those moments, I reimagined all my feelings. Hughes Big Red Girls Basketball team and Barvenia Wooten do it again. We were making history. We were heading to the state tournament, but not before the regional tournament, which left us battling injuries sustained during the regional games."Fairall blames refs for injuries," wrote the Cincinnati Enquirer.

Our head coach, Jamie Fairall, was furious with the officials. The lack of blowing their whistles for aggressive play under the basket left our top defensive player, Marilyn Banks, out with a torn ligament and me with a severely sprained ankle. Banks was out and I was questionable with five days before the state tournament held at the Ohio University in Columbus, Ohio.

There was no way that I was going to sit on the bench. I was going to do anything and everything that I could to be ready to play. I had experienced sprained ankles before; however, this was the most severe. I had to go to therapy twice a day with the hopes that I would be ready to play come Friday, five days later.

In the meantime, as I sat at home nursing my ankle, I received a phone call from the press informing me that I had been named the Associated Press Player of the Year in Class AAA Girls' Basketball. Wow! What an honor. I was quoted in the newspaper the next day, "Hey. Oh. Wow. That is exciting. The swelling is going down right now." College basketball here I come.

With this news, I became even more determined to play. I would soak my ankle in ice in addition to the treatments received from the doctors. Nothing was going to stop me from playing. This was our team's dream and my dream of culminating my senior year with a state title. The possibilities of winning the state tournament were not as bright as we had imagined before. With the two injuries to Marilyn and me, we would have to rely on the backup players. Maybe, just maybe, I might be ready.

> The excitement and enthusiasm that came from scoring the ball was exuberating for me.

Coach Fairall suggested that I stay back to get treatment and join the team on Friday before the game.

Friday was the tip off and the semi-final game between Hughes High School and Barberton High School was underway. As I sat anxiously on the bench with a bandage wrapped ankle on the bench, I couldn't help but wonder when and if I was going to get in the game. The adrenaline was flowing and my team was down at the end of the first quarter. I couldn't take it any longer as I watched my team struggle. I turned to my coach and told her that I was ready to go in and to tape up my ankle, because I was not going to miss this opportunity to fulfill my dream of playing in the state tournament. Despite our efforts and my performance, 23 points, 7 rebounds, etc., we succumbed to Barberton, but not without a fight.

The accolades would continue at the end of the basketball season. In addition to the AP honors, I would be voted United Press International (UPI) Player of the Year for the State of Ohio's Class AAA in girls' basketball. Next, "Wooten named among the top All-City Prep Players of Cincinnati." These were just a few more honors to go with my collection of awards and accomplishments.

The most memorable honor was having the top well-known pizza restaurant in Cincinnati, Buddy LaRosa's, honor me for all my accomplishments. They created a caricature poster of me listing all of my academic and sports achievements. They displayed them in all their restaurants in the Cincinnati area for a week to celebrate and showcase my accomplishments as one of Cincinnati's finest. I was speechless. I remain grateful and thankful to this day.

There was other pivotal moment along my high school journey that helped shape and mold me into the person that I am today. I remember the enjoyment that we experienced during lunchtime. Our school was located directly across from the University of Cincinnati. Our school and the UC were both surrounded by restaurants, delis and a variety of small businesses. We were given 30-minutes for lunch and allowed to leave the premises, but it was mandatory that we returned.

Some of us enjoyed a longer break, because we had a lunch period when we didn't have a class. Sometimes for lunch, we would leave school and buy our lunch at the fast food restaurants. At other times during lunch period, they played music in one of our old cafeterias and we would just dance, dance, dance to the Motown hits.

We thoroughly enjoyed ourselves and we had a blast. This is where we would either learn or teach each other the new steps and dances. We would mimic Soul Train by forming lines, clapping and cheering each other on as we danced down the line. It was awesome. Just thinking about those times makes me smile.

Every day in high school was an experience. Just like my love for education, sports and performing that I had developed and embraced in elementary school, so too was my love and determination as I walked the long halls of Hughes High School, knowing that I was on my path and heading in the right direction. I was fortunate to be an integral part of the success that, as black girls from all different communities, who built a dynasty of winning during my four years at Hughes High School. The cohesiveness and the support for one another would be recognized and celebrated for years to come.

It was our time. I'm reminded of a quote from Dr. Wayne Dyer, "You can't stop a divine idea whose time has come." Our time had come and it was perfect! The universe had long prepared us for this moment. Little did we know our angels were guiding us all along the way, because I believe we went with the flow and didn't resist. We were having too much fun!

As my senior year ended, I had made significant contributions while creating memorable events that will remain with me for the rest of my life. I had left my legacy! I went on to be the treasurer of our senior class and was voted runner up to Homecoming Queen by my peers. I graduated with honors and was ranked 12th out of a class of 420, finishing in the top 10% of my class. What a remarkable achievement to attain along with my athletic success.

The song "Ain't No Stopping Us Now," by McFadden & Whitehead, was our signature song as we closed out our senior year in 1979. "Ain't No Stopping Us Now" was another mantra that I would refer to over and over as motivation to prepare me for my journey through college. There would truly be no stopping me!

I was headed to college and my dreams continued to come true. The foundation for me to succeed in college had been laid. The learning and growth that I had acquired from my experiences and lessons as I progressed through my four years at Hughes High School would pay off royally.

A few years later, I became the first female athlete from Hughes High School to be inducted into the Cincinnati Public Schools Athletic Hall of Fame in 2013. Little did I know at high school graduation, I had become a pioneer, a trailblazer like many others before me, setting the path and opening the doors for others to follow, especially girls. Now it was time to move on and test my skills and talents at the next level. I was nervous, but excited. Only more greatness was to come.

UP & RUNNING 79

AAA Player Of Year Honor Just What 'Beanie' Needed

BY CINDY MORRIS
Enquirer Sports Reporter

Hughes High School's Barvenia ("Beanie") Wooten was ready for some happy news Tuesday.

Upon learning that the Associated Press had named her Player of the Year in Class AAA girls' high school basketball, the 5-foot-8 senior guard responded: "Hey! Oh, Wow! That *is* exciting . . . The swelling is going down right now!"

THAT'S SWELLING as in badly sprained ankle. Wooten suffered the injury Saturday midway through Hughes' victory over Stivers-Patterson in the Southwestern District regional final at Dayton. Although Wooten returned to action after a brief respite, the ankle worsened after the game, and she may not play in Friday's state semifinal against Barberton at Columbus.

But Wooten, an all-A student who has averaged 22 points, 11 re-

play, because her injury is only half of the bad Hughes news.

When Wooten went to the University of Cincinnati's Sports Medicine Institute for therapy Monday, she had company. And when she and *former* starting forward Marilyn Banks appeared at school, they were both on crutches.

BANKS TORE ligaments in her knee during a collision early in the fourth quarter Saturday. She continued to play and didn't feel severe pain until Sunday when she found herself unable to get out of a chair. She will undergo exploratory surgery next Monday. During Monday's practice, the 5-9 senior leaned on her crutches and watched mournfully. "I was looking forward to state," she said. "I was so happy."

Said Hughes coach Janie Fairall, "Now we're at 60% instead of 100%. Even if Beanie's ready, she won't be 100%. Marilyn was one of the key people in our press, one of our top rebounders, one of our quickest peo-

BARVENIA WOOTEN

Banks, who averaged 11 point per game, will be replaced by Venit Mathis, a 5-11 junior. Mathis ha played quite a bit this season as substitute and has averaged 5 points per game. If Wooten doesn play at state, she will be replaced either 5-7 senior Sandy Smith or 5

NAME	POINTS	GRADUATION YEAR
BARVENIA WOOTEN	1,089	1979
LORETTA MELSON	1,040	1983
GAIL ASH	1,380	1986
LINDA MILES	1,144	1997
JASMINE DAVIS	1,169	2009
ALMESHA JONES	1,108	2011

Chapter 5
MY TICKET OUT

After sorting through the overwhelming number of letters of interest that came with offers, I accepted the offer of a full basketball scholarship to attend Virginia Union University. The journey was unfolding. I had defied the odds. I had made it out of the inner city. There were no pregnancies, no criminal records, no baggage and no bad memories or experiences that would hinder my success.

My teammate, Lisa Smith, and I had been flown down on an official visit at the end of our senior year. My decision to attend Virginia Union University would be determined weeks later after returning home to Cincinnati. It was based on a previous conversation that we had had with a football player, Larry Barringer, during our visit. Larry shared with us that the best way to make a decision in choosing the right college "Would be based on whether we wanted to be around our own (black students) or if we preferred to be at a predominately white institution (PWI). At a HBCU you could be a big fish in a small pond, or a small fish in a big pond at a PWI." The choice was mine. I thought being around your own could be better.

As a result of the words of encouragement that I had received from Reverend Jessie Jackson, Dr. Calvert Smith and many other Black mentors

I made my decision to attend VUU, a Historical Black College & University (HBCU). I wanted to follow their advice to help empower and raise the consciousness of my race.

I had this yearning to help my own people, verses attending a predominately white institution. I felt that the PWI only wanted me for my athleticism. I witnessed countless times during my era how PWIs used many of our black athletes for their own personal gain. Unfortunately, at the end of their playing careers the majority returned back to their community no more educated than when they first entered and sadly, without a degree.

Because the veil had been lifted from my eyes about the unfair treatment of black student-athletes at many of the PWI's during my meeting with Dr. Smith, I wanted no part of it. Although I felt confident in my abilities to succeed at either institution, I felt compelled to give my gifts and talents to an HBCU.

Once I had made my decision, Lisa said that she wanted to go where I went. So weeks later, we packed up our things and hit the road. Lisa's high school boyfriend drove us in his company's van.

> Theodore Roosevelt said, "People don't care how much you know, until they know how much you care."

The trip was over 10 hours. With only a few stops, we made it safely to campus a couple of days before orientation. During those days, the large army footlockers were popular. Just about all my belongings fit in that locker. I didn't have much. I was just glad to be in college.

Because I had grown up having my needs met, the little that I had was enough to get me by my first year. During our first year in college, Lisa and I were roommates. After the first two weeks, I was homesick and had thought about going home until I met up with a few students who encouraged me to stay. They told me to give it some time and that I would adjust to this new experience. They were right. My homegirl, Lisa and I began to make friends. We started hanging out with the girls on the basketball team. From that point on, I was hooked. Virginia Union University would now become my home away from home, my new world.

My four years at VUU would almost mirror my four years from high school in terms of how each year unfolded as I continued to evolve. This would be one of the best and most profound decisions that I had ever made in my life. Virginia Union University would become my home for the next four years.

I was intrigued by the upperclassmen, just like I had been in high school. They too walked with confidence. They had a swag that said, "I believe in me." There was a spirit of togetherness even as everyone seemed to move to their own beat, their own rhythm and this aligned with my soul. I could be me. No one judged me because of the color of my skin. We were all in it together. Everyone demonstrated a sense of pride. They felt good about who they were and proudly wore their color. I had not experienced anything like that. I had been told by some of my mentors and others who had attended a black institution about how wonderful it was to be in an environment that embraced our blackness and affirmed our right to exist. They were right!

Freshman year was a wonderful year that set the foundation for all the great things to come and prepared me to achieve my goals, dreams and aspirations. It was awesome. VUU had become my second home. Everyone was so nice, friendly and helpful. The professors were very demanding yet caring. They exemplified what Theodore Roosevelt said, "People don't care how much you know, until they know how much you care." This was not just a slogan for them; they truly cared. They were always directing us and giving us well-needed advice and counseling.

I have fond memories of our Dean of Students, Mrs. Carolyn Daughtry, who passed years after my graduation. She was a beautiful woman of wisdom, inside and out. She was my mother away from home and was always challenging me. She had taken a special interest in me because I had shown her that I was very excited about coming to college and was ready and open to grow and be my best. I shared with her that I was the first and only child in my family to attend college and to have earned a full athletic scholarship.

I normally don't believe in love at first sight. But after my first two weeks at Virginia Union University, I was in love with VUU. It was love at first sight. I believe God has a way of placing you on your path if you trust the process. I did. It would be a very exciting, enthusiastic and challenging experience filled with trials and triumphs.

At that moment, little did I know or realize that my journey through VUU was clear. Years later, I can see how the pattern of my life unfolded. It is as if God had strategically ordained my life and allowed me to fulfill my dreams and aspirations of becoming a great student-athlete at a higher level and a top scholar female athlete.

The atmosphere at VUU was promising. I could feel the vibes as everyone walked with confidence and self-assurance that they were here for a reason and a purpose. There was a distinct movement among these black students that I had never experienced before amongst such a large number of black people in any place, environment or event. I was astonished. It was amazing to see and feel. And I believe VUU was ready for me. Over the next four years, my life would ebb and flow. The biggest challenge that I would experience would come from dating, which I will go into detail later in this chapter.

As a freshman at VUU, we were assigned an upperclassman as our mentor. They would be responsible for helping us navigate college, guide us and assist us with any other needs, to include tutoring, locating resources and how to avoid the pitfalls that come with being a first-time collegiate student miles away from home. After all, they went through this experience too. My mentor was the homecoming queen, Corliss Bailey. She was beautiful, kind and intelligent. I believe her major was business and she was a member of Delta Sigma Theta, the illustrious and prominent organization that I would later join.

Corliss was well respected on our campus and among our peers. I believe God has an interesting way of putting people in your life at the right moment to allow you to see a reflection of who you are becoming. As I reflect, I now see that my path was being shown to me through the life of Corliss. She was very confident and self-assured. I'm unsure if she realized that she made a profound impact on my life. She exemplified all the qualities that, over my next three years at VUU, I would come to realize that I too embodied. These same qualities helped shape and enrich my character. Not only did I go on to be voted homecoming queen my senior year, but I also became a member of the great Delta Sigma Theta Sorority, Beta Epsilon Chapter.

When we take time out of our busy lives to quiet ourselves and listen intently, God has a way of revealing our path and helping us to see whether we are in alignment with our true calling. At that moment, I was in alignment. I felt His presence because of the excitement and joy that I was experiencing. Just like my favorite mantra from high school from that song. Can you hear it? Can you feel it? "Ain't No Stopping Us Now!" We must continue to move forward, even in the face of adversity, because when you are in alignment, there ain't no stopping you!

The late Tricky Harris had recruited us to help rebuild and grow the women's basketball program at VUU. Here I was again, unbeknownst to me, initiating an integral part of

something big and nationally recognized. I and the other great and dynamic players including Maria Nicholson, Paris McWhirter and Veta Williams just to name a few who joined me at the beginning and would leave behind a legacy as National Basketball Champions that no other women's basketball team has achieved thus far.

Coach Tom Harris with (Kneeling) Paris McWhirter, Left, Barvenia Wooten, and Eunice Johnson

Practices were unlike high school. We were now practicing against others who were equally talented, strong, skilled players. We had to earn our right to be on the court. Players were from various places, like New York, Washington DC, Virginia and even Ohio (smile). Again, my dream had come true. During high school, I read about the challenges that many black children had to encounter in some of the impoverished neighborhoods filled with crime, just to survive.

I had expressed to myself that it would be an honor to play with girls from DC and New York, knowing that they too had defied the odds. I believed that they would not only be physically strong, but also mentally strong as well. And they didn't disappoint my belief. Although they were a challenge on the court, off the court, they were very helpful and supportive. Over the season, we built a strong bond. I'm not sure of our record during that year, but I know that they helped me strengthen my game and build my confidence as a collegiate athlete.

If you got knocked down in practice, which sometimes was done purposely, no one would baby you or even offer to pick you up. You had to get up on your own. And to this day, I appreciate, that lesson that I learned. When life knocks you down and sometimes it will, especially if you are not following your right path and your purpose, you must get back up. Literally and figuratively, we have to get up every day.

You see, girls' basketball or girls' sports for that matter, was not very popular and we didn't get the same treatment or resources as our counterparts, the boys. I remember even in high school, it was the same until we started to win. Even that didn't solve some of the inequities that female athletes had experienced and still do even today.

Nevertheless, we had to continue to get up. Just like in high school, I found myself becoming an advocate for our right to receive the same as the men. Being treated like a second-class citizen was how most of us felt. We didn't receive the same attention or support as the men's programs. Why should they get more recognition when we were involved in some of the same sports?

We practiced and trained as hard as they did, we sacrificed our time, dedicated our talents and gifts to the same organization. We should then, on all accounts, have received the same resources. We too had earned and deserved to be treated equally. But we weren't.

Despite these challenges, I was madly in love with Virginia Union University. VUU could do no wrong. Virginia Union University had developed a strong reputation for having one of the most winning athletic programs in our conference, the CIAA. The CIAA was one of the top premier black conferences in the country, especially for basketball. We had developed a confidence in ourselves and no one was going to stop us. The women's basketball team would be one of those programs.

Over the next few years, the women's basketball team would make a remarkable turnaround, winning two CIAA Conference Championships back to back 1981 & 1982, and the only NCAA Division II National Women's Basketball Championship at VUU on record.

The campus was buzzing and our football team was one of the top programs in our conference. Coming to college, I had not been a football fan. My high school team was not good and therefore I don't remember ever going to the games. However, one day as I was hanging out in my freshman dorm room with some of my friends, we suddenly heard the bus carrying the football players onto campus. They were loud and excited. They had won another game. For some strange reason, I was hooked.

Then, out of the clear blue sky, several young men converged in front of my dorm, performing and stepping as they shouted various chants. They were the men of Omega Phi Psi, one of the Greek fraternities on campus. This would be my first experience seeing a live performance as I watched them move to a beat and rhythm that was characteristic of the Greeks at HBCUs. Now, I was really hooked. Is this what the college life experience was? If so, I was all in. We were screaming and calling out to them as they performed. Their movements were electrifying as they moved in unison. The rhythm and the beat resonated with my soul. I wanted to be a part of this life. It was invigorating!

Again, my quest for fulfilling my purpose for being was revealed as I watched in amazement. In that moment I was suspended in time. My total being was in ecstasy. This is where I was supposed to be. I was in alignment with my purpose. It felt good. I believe that when we have this type of experience that connects to our soul, we should recognize that we are headed in the right direction and on our path.

Delta Sigma Theta Sorority Inc., here I come. After the showcase was over, the excitement among us continued into a discussion about our individual decision to join a Greek organization. There were many to consider, such as Alpha Kappa Alpha Sorority, Delta Sigma Theta Sorority, Zeta Phi Beta or Sigma Gamma Rho. I decided that Delta Sigma Theta would be me! As I had observed how the women of Delta carried themselves on campus, strong, powerful, beautiful and very confident, I knew beyond a shadow of a doubt that I wanted to be a Delta! I would have to wait for my sophomore year to explore that.

There was a pivotal moment that happened at the end of my freshman season that would confirm again that I was on the right path. Some of the players got together to discuss a few situations that were happening within our team and the coach. Everyone agreed that at our team meeting we would all share our concerns. I was excited and ready. I felt everyone had each other's back, until it was time to speak. Unfortunately, I found myself alone. Suddenly no one had anything to say. Now, I was standing there alone.

At first, I felt betrayed and then fearful. For some strange reason, I felt compelled to speak. Maybe they were not brave enough and fearful that the coach would bench them. However, I had promised myself that I would speak up for others and myself whenever possible. And this time would be no different.

My angels were with me and I felt God's presence as I began to express my (our) concerns. It was not about me. It was about standing up for what I believed and how speaking up can help the well-being of all involved. I would experience the repercussions of my decision over the next couple of games. These repercussions, I believe, are what had prevented my teammates from speaking up earlier. Nevertheless, how long would I be willing to be benched because of my right to speak up?

I met with Coach Harris, who was also the Athletic Director and assuming the role of assistant coach, to discuss the issue. Coach Harris had become like a father to me. I believed he was one of my angels. I didn't go into detail about the conversation, but I did tell him that I would not be returning to VUU next year. I was not going to accept being reprimanded for speaking up. It was against my character and beliefs. I told him that it was not about me demanding playing time if I didn't earn it, but it was about being benched because I spoke up about an issue that was truly affecting the team. A few days later I was back on the court. Apparently, he had spoken to the head coach and the coach's attitude changed.

I was hungrier than ever to prove my point on the court. I would not bow down to make someone feel better about their indiscretions. I was there to succeed and refused to let anything, person or situation deter me. Remember, God gave us all a voice! It is solely up to us to use it.

So, at the end of the school year, I decided to leave. I met with Coach Harris and informed him of my decision. Although we had rectified the issue, I didn't feel comfortable about playing for a coach whose actions, in my opinion, were not in alignment with his words. I thanked Coach Harris for the opportunity and expressed that I knew I wasn't irreplaceable. I'm sure they would find another player. It was not all about me and yet it was. I didn't want to take that chance of staying another year to see if the head coaches' actions were sincere.

Coach Harris always told me that I was wise for my age. He couldn't believe how well I had expressed myself and while he tried to encourage me to stay, he asked me to think about my decision and confirm with him before I left for the summer.

And then, weeks before I left for the summer, here came tall, dark and handsome, Robert Collier Sr. He was a football player inquiring about my number. Over the course of my freshman year, I had dated a couple of guys. Nothing serious. Now that I was ready to leave, he wanted to get to know me. I told him I was not planning to come back, but he wanted to keep in touch anyway.

Now remember, back in the '80s, we only had house phones. There were no cells phones, pagers or computers for that matter. During those days, we communicated a lot by writing letters to each other. Yes and we would explode with excitement as we pulled the letters out of the mailbox. And the letters would be followed by a phone call, which would last hours until either your parents or siblings needed the phone.

We had some time to get to know each other over the next couple of weeks as we waited for parents to mail the money for transportation home. Imagine that. No debit cards, cash apps, access to banks in another state, etc. The only option to get money quicker was by telegram through Western Union. We exchanged numbers and addresses and agreed to keep in touch.

"Beanie," I heard someone calling me as I walked across campus. It was Coach Harris. He asked me to come to his office, because he had some great news to share with me. At first, I was hesitant. I had made up my mind. I was transferring. "Great news!" exclaimed Coach Harris. Virginia Union University had decided to let go of all part-time employees who coached. You had to be full-time to coach.

At that time, I don't think some of the coaches, especially the female sports, were full-time paid positions. As a result, the Head Coach was released and Coach Harris was taking over the program as the new Head Coach, since he was a full-time employee. I had mixed emotions. Although, I felt relieved, I didn't give him an immediate answer.

I asked him to give me some time over the next couple of weeks and I would call him and give him my decision. I would finish my freshman year academically strong with a 3.8 GPA. However, I would leave having to make a major decision regarding the life of my basketball career at VUU. I knew time would tell. The money had finally arrived and I was headed home for the summer. I thought being at home would allow me to clear my thoughts and not feel pressure to finalize my decision. I was excited to be back home for the summer. I was happy to see my family and friends. I continued working on my game, playing with the guys at the area playgrounds, as usual.

I had made a name for myself and all the neighborhood boys wanted to challenge me. I looked forward to playing against them. Just about every Saturday morning, or sometimes in the late evenings after work, I would hustle out to the playgrounds eager for a game of basketball. I was both enthused and humbled to be one of the people picked as we formed teams of five.

I can remember it, like it was just yesterday. The adrenaline was flowing and I was caught up in the moment. This was my heaven. Time didn't exist and I didn't want this moment to end. Again, I knew that I was connected with my soul's purpose and desires. There was no stopping me now. I felt the power within and felt that I was born for sports.

Who said that because I was a girl I should be in the house cooking, sewing and playing with dolls? No, I was here to defy the stereotypes and limitations that were placed on girls across all walks of life. Who said we must accept the roles that society has written for females? Not Barvenia Michelle Wooten!

I believe that strong athletic women were born to help eradicate these old mindsets and change the way the world sees women. It was with this belief and mindset that I was determined to show not only the boys, the world, and all those who thought that girls couldn't play competitive basketball that they were wrong.

The summer had been good and was coming to an end. Sophomore year was upon me and it was time to make my decision. I decided to return to VUU. My decision to return was based on a few thought-provoking questions I had to ask myself. Do I give up now and lose one year of eligibility and the progress that I made athletically and academically? Do I want to leave behind the friendships with teammates and others? Was it worth starting over? Would I allow one unwelcomed situation to overshadow the great moments and positive experiences I had?

Just like my sophomore year in high school, my sophomore year in college would be the defining moment of my college career. I was ready to go back to college, VUU, I'm back!

As the season started, I was ready, eager and enthused about applying the new skills and toughness that I had learned from playing the neighborhood boys over the summer. Many of them were home from college as well. My ability to compete with them increased my confidence and mental toughness. Because of my growth and increased passion for the game, I would become one of the top players on my team in scoring and rebounding. All my hard work, perseverance and faith in my abilities would pay off. I would begin to make a name for myself as a standout student athlete.

Several times I was recognized as player of the week and would eventually make the All-CIAA Conference team. During the season, I decided to take on my desire to become a member of Delta Sigma Theta that I had expressed to myself during my freshman year. After finding out more about the purpose of being a member of the organization, I needed and wanted to be an asset to my community through volunteerism.

As mentioned before, these women commanded attention and respect as they walked the campus. You could tell, they were confident in who they were. The vibe that I felt spoke to my soul. I felt that I embodied these same characteristics and I wanted to not only experience and become a member of this dynamic and powerful organization, but also to join and contribute to this beautiful sisterhood. Joining Delta Sigma Theta would be a great outlet to give back to others.

I liked the idea that Greek organizations at HBCU's were committed to serving the community through various volunteering throughout the campus and surrounding community. In the fall of my first semester of my sophomore year, I submitted my application and later received the great news that I had been accepted.

My life as a student-athlete would continue to blossom. Weeks before accepting the invitation, I had a thorough conversation with my coach. I explained to him my reasons for joining. I wanted to help make a difference by helping others through volunteering in the community and Delta would provide me with the opportunity to fulfill my passion for helping others. Our agreement was that as long as I made it to practices and attended all my classes, he would support my decision. But if I failed to meet these obligations, I would have to quit the line, because I was on full scholarship and my academics and basketball were my primary obligations.

I made line for Delta Sigma Theta. Making line was a process that required the prospective members to complete a rigorous training program for eight-weeks before receiving full membership into the organization.

My training was more than I could ever have imagined. It was intense.

We were required to learn the history and founders. We learned to organize and prepare ourselves individually and as a group the night before. We were taught valuable lessons of working together and holding each other accountable. I learned some things about myself. I was mentally stronger than I thought. I had come to know that there was truly something special about me. This knowing became so deep that words could not express the revelation.

My pledge period was a great experience.

It shaped my life and helped build my character. I learned so much from being on line. We learned the true definition of sisterhood and how important it was to support each other, regardless of the circumstances. We had to support each other in every aspect during the pledge period—academically, mentally, socially, psychologically and spiritually.

There was no such thing as not being there to support your line sister. Most importantly, we learned how to think on our feet, present ourselves in a very dignified and professional manner and "Never Use Excuses." Either you got it done or you didn't. "No Excuses" would become one of the driving forces that taught me how to effectively use my time wisely, value my opportunities and strategically balance and manage the many roles I took on as a student-athlete at VUU. Delta Sigma Theta had brought out the best in me.

Junior year we headed for Conference Championship #2. The team had gelled and we were on a mission. There was silence in the arena with a few minutes before halftime. Our attention was directed toward our bench. Our beloved head coach, Tricky Tom Harris, had fallen to the floor. In that moment we didn't know what had happened.

The assistant coaches gathered us together and ushered us into the locker room. Coach Harris had collapsed and suffered a heart attack. As we sat in the locker room, everyone was quietly trying to figure out what had occurred. We were in shock. What were we going to do? Our assistant coach informed us that he was just as shocked as we were and that he would leave the decision up to us whether we wanted to continue the game. We all decided that Coach Harris would have wanted us to play and that we did. We won the game and conference title in his honor.

The interesting fact is that we were up by one point before he collapsed and we won by one point. Although, they didn't tell us until later the next day that Coach Harris had passed, I believe he was our sixth man and as our angel, helped us win the game.

The ride back to the campus was somber. I couldn't help but reflect on how much Coach Harris meant to me. He had sacrificed so much of his time and effort in building the women's sports teams during his tenure. Life on campus was going to be different and a big adjustment. I had lost another father.

This time was different. Having never known my first father before he died, I believe God had granted me the opportunity to experience what it was like to have a father in Coach Harris. The only other father figure was Dr. Calvert Smith. He had been instrumental in opening my eyes and raising my understanding and awareness about racism and discrimination that was happening all around me.

A memorial was held on campus for Coach Harris and as one of the team captains, I was chosen to say a few words and read Scripture. I felt a deep loss. However, Coach Harris's legacy, teachings and the lessons that he taught us would leave an imprint on my life. One of the most memorable events was seeing him enjoy a hearty laugh with one of the giants of men's basketball in the world of the CIAA, Clarence Big House Gains, as they chatted before one of our double-header games with the men's teams.

Coach Harris always encouraged us to give back once we had graduated. I believe my sense of urgency and valuing time came from the teachings of Coach Harris. I can still hear him saying to us all the time, even now as I write this book, "Take advantage of time and don't worry about sleeping because you'll have enough time to sleep once your life has ended." Every time I think or feel like I should be sleeping more than awake pursuing my dreams and goals, I can hear Coach Harris in my mind reminding me that I'll have plenty of time to sleep.

Decades later, I would come back to be the head coach at my alma mater,

Barvenia Wooten, "we dedicated game to Harris."

by Pettigrew Royal

Barvenia Wooten started playing basketball in the ninth grade. "After volleyball season was over there was nothing else to do. So me and a girlfriend decided to go out for the basketball team." Before that she was never really interested in basketball, she only played volleyball and softball. "My first year playing basketball was so exciting to me. That following summer I was always outside with the fellas learning basketball skills and rules."

At Union Wooten sees the practice sessions as more than just running and shooting, "practice involves a lot of education." And maybe it was that education that took them to the NCAA Championship. Wooten feels "the bench coming in and backing up the starters is what earned them the Championship."

Every women on the Pantherette squad earned their championship.

Wooten, "We had nothing to lose, but a lot was gained."

Williams congratulates Wooten after she hits the first of two free throws.

VUU and be honored to speak at the commissioning of our Fitness Center on his behalf. Coach Harris will always be a part of my life and my legacy. I am grateful to have had the pleasure and honor to play for such a great human being. He was always giving. As my junior year was coming to an end, it was bittersweet. I would miss Coach Harris dearly. He would always call me by a special version of my name because he could never pronounce my name correctly. But I enjoyed hearing him mess up my name. I had lost a father, mentor and a friend.

After winning our second CIAA Conference back-to-back, we would lose in the second round of the NCAA Division II Regional Championship. We vowed that next year we would go all the way and win the national championship. And we did.

I also fulfilled my dream of following in the footsteps of my freshman mentor, Miss Corliss Bailey and be voted by my peers as the 1983 Miss Virginia Union University. Again, I believe that this was no coincidence. My freshman mentor was Miss Virginia Union and during my sophomore year, I was crowned Miss Sophomore.

During my junior year, I managed the campaign for one of the Miss Virginia Union candidates Matoka Waller after candidates and we successfully won. My purpose for running for these positions was all about leadership.

Senior year would be the best year of my collegiate experience, just like my senior year of high school. Could this be possible? My formal education, my achievements in sports and holding leadership positions in high school would be synonymous in college.

My life repeated itself in both groups of four years, but at a greater experience finishing strong with many achievements and accomplishments that would be remembered and recognized for many years to come, even up to this moment.

Just like my senior year in high school, I graduated with honors, cum laude with a degree in Accounting. I was treasurer of my senior class in high school and treasurer of my chapter's sorority. I was runner up for Homecoming Queen in high school and in college, Miss Virginia Union 1983. My team advanced to the championship tournaments, losing in the semi-final game of the Ohio Girls' Basketball AAA State Tournament in high school, but yet, finished at the pinnacle of my collegiate basketball career, winning the NCAA Division II National Women's Basketball Championship.

I earned ESPN's Most Vitalis Award, finishing the game with 25 points and grabbing 15 rebounds. I was headed for professional women's basketball. The spring of my junior year at VUU (prior to my senior year), I was crowned "Miss Virginia Union University" for the upcoming year in 1983. One of my privileges during that Miss VUU reign of 1983 was the rare opportunity to meet the beautiful and lovely wife of Dr. Martin Luther King, Jr., Coretta Scott King. In fact, I was privileged to be her personal escort.

As the queen, my responsibilities included escorting all dignitaries, especially women, during their visit on campus. When Mrs. King came to visit our campus in December 1982, with great humility and enthusiasm, I had the honor and privilege of escorting her throughout her entire visit on campus. It was an honor and a privilege. I will treasure this experience for the rest of my life.

December 10, 1982

Coretta On Campus

Students welcome Mrs. King as she arrives on campus.

She was a beautiful, caring and dynamic woman. There was a great presence about Mrs. King. She was very confident and assuring. Her presence and speech sent vibrations through all who were present. I will always be grateful for the opportunity to have met such a powerful and iconic woman. She absolutely inspired me!

Once again, I was excited and enthused about taking my skills to the next level. I wanted to play basketball as long as my body would hold up.

Chapter 6
THE PURSUIT OF BALANCE

Caps were flying high in the air; tears streamed down our faces; parents, family and friends shouted congratulations as we walked across the stage to receive our degrees. Our degrees were the key to opening the first of many doors. It was time. I was transitioning to the next chapter of my life after a wonderful, exciting and illustrious career at Virginia Union University. I wondered, would the next four years of my life resemble that of the eight years of major accomplishments, awards and achievements that I had garnered in both high school and in college? Well, almost.

After college, I was left with my dream of going overseas to play professional basketball or maybe the Olympics. During my junior year, Coach Harris and I had talked a great deal about him helping and preparing me to go overseas. He had contacts and assured me that once I graduated, he would facilitate the process. Unfortunately, I would not be able to benefit from our plan, since he was now gone and there was no one else that I could turn to for assistance.

A few calls here and there came up empty. But I didn't give up. As always, I was determined to exhaust every avenue that I could to manifest my dream of playing professional women's basketball. I asked around and discovered that the U.S Olympics would be having tryouts for the 1987 Pan American Games, the year before the 1988 Olympics.

I was puzzled to find out players from programs other than Division I were not afforded an invitation and/or selected to play for the U.S. National Teams and/or Olympics. This was a whole new world for me. I had not been aware, or knowledgeable, about how the Pan American Games, Olympics or USA National Basketball teams operated. All I knew was that I was willing to do whatever I had to do in order to play in the Olympics.

I was baffled as to why other programs, like Division II, were not aware of this opportunity. I don't recall my high school coaches sharing this information with us either. The national teams have several age groups and I would have at least qualified for an opportunity to tryout. With this new and exciting information in tow, I would, over the next few years, aggressively train and challenge myself more than ever before.

> The voice on the other end shared the results with excitement and enthusiasm.

After graduation, I decided to stay in Richmond and train. Well, I also decided to stay, because I was in love with my college sweetheart, Robert Collier, who I affectionately called "Bob" as did most everyone. He would be the man I would marry a year later and who would become the father of my two beautiful children over the next four years.

In the meantime, my coach, Lou Hearn, who had taken over the program after the passing of Coach Harris, offered me the opportunity to join the team as an assistant coach, pay me a stipend and provide on-campus housing. Little did I know that this would be the beginning of my coaching career. I never envisioned myself coaching. My dreams were to play basketball for the US Olympics, play professionally, and travel the world as a motivational speaker.

I wanted to inspire and encourage others, especially our youth, to follow their dreams. I wanted them to believe that they have the power within themselves to accomplish their goals. I wanted them to understand that no one could stop them but them. Mostly, I wanted them to know that we all are born with gifts and talents and are destined for greatness.

I was assigned as the Acting Dorm Director for one of the freshman dorms on Newman Hall campus. Ironically, this dorm had been my freshman dorm. Again, my life had come full circle. I was right back where I started. This time, I was functioning in a different capacity. I was now responsible for overseeing the freshman and providing them with guidance and how to navigate their first year in college just like the upperclassmen and dorm director had done for me. This arrangement served me well.

I had a place to live, eat on campus, train and keep close to my love of basketball. During the day, I found temporary jobs while I pursued permanent work to take care of my everyday expenses. I had started an internship with one of the big eight accounting firms Anderson, Cooper & Lybrand in Richmond right before graduating.

During the '80s, accounting firms were large multinational firms and having an accounting degree, this is where you wanted to work. It was very competitive and tough to get in, especially if you were black (minority as they called it during those days). Nevertheless, I was excited. I had landed this position through our Career and Placement Department at VUU. And then, several weeks later it ended. This would be my first face-to-face experience with discrimination in the work world. The Dean of our Accounting School, Dr. Ruth Harris, the first Black woman to pass the CPA (Certified Public Accounting) exam, which was very hard to do the first time, had informed us about discrimination.

She had encouraged a group of us accounting majors to take the CPA exam to get experience, with the hope of passing at least three of the parts as required during that time. And now, I was confronted with this thing called discrimination. If you didn't look like or act like them, you didn't belong. I wondered why? Aren't we all created in the image of God? What makes the color of your skin better than anyone else? I was left with the notion that I would be denied a full-time position for the job of my dreams just because of the color of my skin and not because of the content of my character. I had met the qualifications of the position. What would be the reason?

My supervisor had called to inform me that I had been selected to attend the 90 days of on-the-job training and scheduled our meeting. When I arrived, he was excited and happy to meet me. He directed me to go meet with Human Resources to complete the employment documents. My degree in accounting had paid off and I was headed for a career in accounting. I was nervous, but excited. I had a job with one of the top prestigious accounting firms in the country, or at least I thought.

As a black girl graduating from a histocailly black college/university (HBCU), it would be a major achievement. I can only speculate that I would have been among the few minorities who were hired and would have had the honor of dispelling stereotypes, myths and negative views about the character, intelligence and work ethic of African Americans as perceived by other races. As quickly as I began working for Anderson, Cooper & Lybrand, as a black girl from the inner city of Cincinnati, graduate of a HBCU in a predominately white environment, my employment there would become a distant memory.

As I introduced myself to the woman in HR who was white, her facial expression said it all. "You are not who I expected you to be. You are black." Maybe because of my name, Barvenia Wooten, she couldn't decipher my race or ethnicity. I was shocked because this was my first encounter with her. I didn't like the look on her face. For a moment time stood still as we both processed our feelings. Both trying to figure out what just occurred.

Once we both returned to reality, she told me in so many words, because you are black, she would not proceed with the hiring process. She would get back to me later. At that very moment, discrimination was surreal. What was I going to do? Who could I talk to? How could I explain what had happened and wondered if I would have this opportunity again? I left with mixed feelings; my emotions were all over the place and it took me a moment to process what had just occurred.

Have you ever experienced a time where you knew that you had prepared yourself and knew that you were qualified, but you were denied because of the color of your skin? How did you handle it? How had the experience prepared you for the next time you would probably have to face this injustice again? Until that moment, I was certain that my education would speak for itself. I believed if I was disciplined and worked hard that I would be given a chance based on my credentials as opposed to being dismissed based on the pigmentation of my skin.

Teachers, mentors, parents, friends, the world, told me that if I followed the process, went to college, got a degree, and graduated, I should land a job in my field of study if I met the qualifications of the position. I did. Although I was told about the ugliness of discrimination, I thought that by following the process I would be exempt and somehow treated differently. I can't say that I was surprised that they never called me back.

It was now time to move forward. This one event was not going to stop me or make me question my abilities. Because of my strong will and determination, I refused to let this situation define me. And this situation only made me more determined as I continued to seek jobs in the accounting field in lieu of my previous encounter.

Virginia Union University had truly prepared me to face the world. VUU had helped me affirm who I was and to believe in my abilities, regardless of the color of my skin. Weeks later I signed up with a temp agency who found work for me at various banks and mortgage companies within the Richmond area.

In the meantime, I was still training with the hope of playing professional basketball either for the Olympics or to go play overseas. I wasn't aware of any local professional teams. Months later, I would land my first job as a Claims Representative for the Department of Health and Human Services in Washington, DC. I went home to spend time with my family in Ohio before returning to DC.

While in DC, one of my college teammates allowed me to stay at her home until my training started. During that time, she introduced me to her women's basketball team, Ted's Elite of the American Amateur Union (AAU) in Washington, DC. I thought this would be a great way for me to improve and increase my chances for getting picked up by the Olympics or exposure to go overseas. So, I joined the team. This would be the beginning of a 15-year basketball career playing with several professional women's basketball teams, including the now defunct American Basketball League (ABL).

The league that we played in was very competitive and I enjoyed every moment. I was on my way! Then the unexpected happened. Two months later while in training for the Federal Government, I would find out that I was pregnant. Could this be happening? I wasn't expecting to have a child before marriage and certainly not at age 22. I recall sitting in my hotel room waiting for the results of my test. And then the phone rang. Before answering the call, I braced myself. Deep down inside, I knew the results.

The voice on the other end shared the results with excitement and enthusiasm. It was as if she had found out that she was expecting. After I hung up the phone, I took a deep breath. My mind raced of what the future would hold. I had never believed in abortions, although, I must admit, the thought did play out in my mind. Why now? I was sure that I had protected myself by taking contraceptives. Was this my fate? After all of the sacrifices I had made, it surely wasn't in my plans. Now what? Would my basketball career come to a screeching halt or would it just be a timeout?

After college, I had no immediate plans of starting a family. If I didn't get a chance to play professional basketball, I would pursue my dream of going to Los Angeles, California and hang out on the beaches for a year. As I saw it, I would be a beach bum, skating, swimming, playing beach volleyball and taking it all in with no intentions other than enjoying my life as a free spirit. Decades later this dream would come true to some degree.

I picked up the phone to call my then boyfriend, Robert Collier, to give him the news that I was expecting his child. He was my college sweetheart. We had dated off and on throughout my four years at VUU. We had no immediate plans to marry after college. We spoke for a while. I was still in shock. We agreed to meet later to discuss our plans. We married on April 6, 1984, months after the birth of our first child.

During my first visit with my OBGYN doctor, I was assured that I could continue to play through my second trimester. I continued to play up through the fifth month of my pregnancy. During those days, we were told that the baby was well protected and that very little harm could be done throughout the second trimester. So, with information in hand, I continued playing until I was elbowed in my side as I came down from a rebound.

This was my warning sign to stop playing and I did. However, because I was just a year out of college and still very much in shape, I swam and did a

> **Everything that I imagined exceeded my expectations.**

little jogging up through the last month of my pregnancy. That's how determined I was to stay in shape and possibly minimize all pain that comes from giving birth. Unfortunately, for me I felt every pain.

It was a boy! Robert Collier, Jr., born September 15, 1984 at 8:42 AM, just short of nine pounds. He was eight pounds, eleven ounces to be exact. At 22 inches long, he was the first of my only two children. His father and my mother pranced around the delivery room at the sight of this large beautiful baby boy. We were delighted at the sight of this new bundle of joy.

During my six-week checkup, I was cleared to resume my activities. I immediately began training and preparing myself to rejoin my women's basketball team. I was ready. I was back to the court with baby and all. Robert Jr. would be the joy of my life over the next three and a half years. Motherhood was both challenging and joyful.

As a young mother, I had to make the adjustments to my life quickly. Robert Jr. was a busy boy and would often attend practices or a game or two with me as I continued to play basketball, believing that I would not stop until I had fulfilled my dream of playing professional basketball. My faith was strong and I always believed that God gives us the desires of our heart.

Months later after the birth of my son, I would receive the news that I was being inducted into the Communiplex Hall of Fame in Cincinnati, Ohio along with Cheryl Miller, Olympic gold medalist in basketball, and several other standout athletes like Flora Jean "Flo" Hyman, an Olympic silver medalist. She played professional volleyball in Japan and succumbed to heart failure during a game. This would be the first of the next four Hall of Fames that I would be inducted in over the next 30 years of my life. I was ecstatic.

With the whole family in tow, we drove up to Cincinnati for the awards presentation. This inner-city girl who had continued to pursue her dreams was now coming home to be recognized once again. What an honor and a privilege it was to be recognized for the hard work, determination and commitment that I had made throughout the years. This honor meant so much to me, because not only was I being recognized, but my family as well.

I had been the first to graduate from high school and college and it was befitting to have the opportunity to come back home to celebrate with family and friends who had continued to believe in me and supported me on this journey. It was a moment I'll cherish as I was able to celebrate with my family. I was filled with joy. Sharing it with the people I loved most meant everything to me. I believe this motivated some of my family members to realize that they too, are capable of achieving great things. My family continues to support me and gets excited every time I achieve a milestone and I do the same for them.

When I returned home from the momentous occasion, to my surprise, as I removed the mail from my mailbox, there was a letter from the Olympic Committee. It was an invitation from the 1987 Olympic Committee to try out for the 1988 Pan American Games.

Could this be happening? Was my dream of playing in the Olympics finally about to manifest? I was ecstatic! The adrenaline was flowing! This little girl who had always followed her dreams was given the opportunity to fulfill her desires and wishes like so many times before. It was unbelievable. I was on my way to train at the Olympic Center in Colorado Springs, Colorado.

Have you ever experienced a time in your life where you realized later that what you wished and dreamed for had come true? Those moments were real and are a personal testimony to never give up on your dreams. Moments like this should give us hope and increase our faith that God, the Divine, has given us the power within us to create our life the way we envision. For those who believe in the Word, Jesus reminded us that we were born to do greater things than he had.

I collected my thoughts, settled myself, and called my mom to share the great news with her. She congratulated me and told me how proud and happy she was for me. I then asked if she could come and assist me with the care of Robert, Jr., I would be away at training for seven to eight days depending on the results. Her answer was a resounding "Yes!" I was ecstatic and overjoyed.

Now that the opportunity had presented itself, for a moment, I questioned whether I was ready. You know how sometimes in life when the thing that you have been wishing for comes true, there is a moment when you ask, "Am I ready? Have I prepared myself?"

> Because of my strong will and determination, I refused to let this situation define me.

That's called doubt and negative self-talk. And if we are not careful, we will talk ourselves right out of the opportunity. I believe this is the reason many people fail and allow the fear of failure to immobilize them. We must guard our minds against negativity. We must keep our eyes on the prize and continue to move forward.

With the news in hand, I needed to find someone or some organization or company to sponsor me. I was responsible for my airfare and transportation from the hotel to the training center. They would cover my hotel and food. After much prayer, calling on various organizations to support me and encouragement from my family, I was fortunate to receive funding from the National Council of Negro Women, Inc., founded by the late Dorothy Heights. I had to go before their Community Outreach Committee and present my story. They were happy for me and agreed to be my sponsor.

My ability to ask for help (overcoming fear of rejection) in the pursuit of my goals and dreams would become one of my many assets. This mindset allowed me to develop the strength and courage to conquer the many challenges and adversities that I had and would continue to experience on this journey. I remain grateful and thankful for their support in helping me pursue my opportunity to play for the Olympics.

My experience at the Pan American Games was a dream come true.

Everything that I imagined exceeded my expectations. There I was in the heart of the highest level of basketball for girls and women. All the top players and renowned coaches during the '80s were there.

Cheryl Miller could not participate because she had blown out her knee. During those days, medical technology wasn't as advanced as it is today. This would be the second of the three times that she and I would meet. The third time I will share later. There were also the McGhee twins, Cynthia Cooper from USC, Teresa Edwards, and Lynette Woodard, who was the first woman to play with the Harlem Globe Trotters. and Lisa Leslie. Included in this group were legendary coaches, Pat Summit, Kay Yow and C. Vivian Stringer. I was in basketball heaven. I really wanted to make the team; unfortunately, I got cut either the second or third round. Nevertheless, I was pleased.

The experience was unbelievable. Three years out of college and after giving birth to my first child, I was able to compete against some of the best women basketball players in the country and I held my own. Was I disappointed that I didn't make the team? Absolutely yes, but not defeated. Again, I had defied all odds. To be given this opportunity was all that I had asked for. To make the team was based on my performance. I had perseverance and regardless of the outcome, I had won. The experience was encouraging. Without any doubt, I knew deep down in my heart that one day I would fulfill my dream of playing professional basketball.

I returned from the Pan American basketball tryouts and rejoined my team, Ted's Elite. Because of the training and playing countless number of games with these top talented women athletes, my individual skills had tremendously improved.

During the second year of playing with Ted's Elite, I found myself expecting my second child. I would play for only two months during that pregnancy, unlike the five months with Robert, Jr. Every pregnancy is different. I had come to believe, as I carried this little soul who would be named Vicki, she attempted to control me throughout the entire pregnancy up until the time she was delivered.

I remember telling my coach that I was six weeks pregnant and that he should limit my playing time to allow me to recuperate between the three to possibly four games that we would play over two days. Unfortunately, after the first day of playing two games, the next morning I could barely move. My body ached and I was sore.

I informed my coach that I would not return to the team until after having my baby. It was a tough decision for me mentally, but physically, I was unable to continue. All I wanted to do during this pregnancy was read and write in my journals. I didn't want to be bothered most of the time. My mom had come to stay with me, as usual and often reminded me of my constant mood swings, which were uncharacteristic of me. I jokingly said, "This little soul was taking over my body and she needed to come out."

I was in the delivery room on July 18, 1988, at approximately 11:46 PM.

"Did you know the sex of your child?" asked the doctor.

"Yes, I believe it's a girl," I replied. A few months earlier, Spirit had revealed to me that I was carrying a girl.

"Guess what?" exclaimed my doctor, "It's a girl."

I had changed her name three times before deciding to name her Vicki Michelle Collier. She was named after my favorite music artist, Vicki Wayans and my middle name, Michelle. She would be my last child and would follow in my footsteps. Once again, after my six-week checkup and cleared by my doctor, I was back on the court.

A few months after Vicki was born, I was inducted into my second Hall of Fame. This time, by my alma mater, Virginia Union University. VUU inducted me, along with two of my other teammates, Maria and Paris. I believe we were among the first females to be inducted into VUU's Hall of Fame for our contributions for winning back-to-back conference championships in 1981 and 1982.

We also were the first black college to win a Division II National Championship in 1983 and even after I graduated, they finished as the 1984 National Championship runner-up. I was in awe! The recognition of all my past achievements, as a result of my commitment to basketball and always giving my best, was being honored.

Both my children would go on to play basketball, beginning with the little leagues, Boys and Girls Clubs, AAU, middle and high school and all the way up to the collegiate level. I would have the distinct opportunity to coach both up through high school and coach Vicki in college and professionally. With Robert Jr., standing at 6'5", a lefty with the classic jumper, I thought at least he would have an opportunity to play basketball overseas. However, after two years in college, his path would take on a different direction and give me my first two beautiful grandchildren, Khai & Sanaa. Not Vicki. Standing at 5'11",  graceful around the basket, excellent rebounder and very talented, she would continue to play like her mom all the way up to the professional level.

Robert and Vicki both would garner many awards for their outstanding achievements in all the sports that they played, mainly basketball. Both would earn full basketball scholarships, Robert at Elizabeth City State University and Vicki at Old Dominion and my alma mater, Virginia Union. It would an honor and a privilege to coach them both, especially Vicki in college at my alma mater.

As Head Coach at Virginia Union University she would help me to win the 2012 CIAA Northern Division Championship and I would get Coach of the Year and she would make the first team All CIAA Conference team. A feat that I believe no mother and daughter has accomplished in the history of the Central Intercollegiate Athlete Association to date.

As a wife, mother and professional, I took on many roles. The ability to balance and keep my family functioning was a daily task. In between fulfilling my roles, somehow, I was able to find time for my own personal extra-curricular activities of playing on volleyball and softball teams. I refused to allow anything to discourage me from doing the things that I enjoyed the most, even with having a family. Life is short and we don't know how many days we have here on earth. I've always valued time; it is a precious commodity and you can't get time back. Time is always moving forward with you or without you.

I believe that we are accountable for our time here on earth. I am reminded of something Muhammed Ali said, "Don't count the days. Make the days count." How we use every second, minute, hour or moment of the day will determine how we live and how our life and legacy will be defined and remembered.

A few years later as I was working at home, my home phone rang, "May I speak with Barvenia Wooten?" said the voice on the other end of the phone.

"This is she," I replied.

"We are calling from the Central Intercollegiate Athletic Association." This CIAA was the basketball conference for which we had won the back-to-back championships. "We are calling to congratulate you on being inducted into the CIAA Hall of Fame, along with two of your teammates, as one of the 25 greatest women's basketball players in the history of women's basketball in the CIAA of 1999."

I was speechless. I couldn't wait to tell my family! My children, Robert Jr. and Vicki jumped with excitement as I told them about the induction. To them, their mother was a star. I could see the gleam in their eyes as they tried to comprehend what it all really meant. They would find out later on when they had shared the news with all their friends in the neighborhood and in school. They were proud of their mother and I was overjoyed that I had this moment to share with them. Another induction. I was elated. My soul rejoiced and I danced in celebration of this honor. I was a trailblazer.

I shared the news with all my family and friends. Some were happy for me and some were proud of me, but those who knew me well expressed how deserving I was of this award; I was honored and humbled. All I've ever desired is that my life would become an inspiration to help others to follow their dreams until fulfillment. My legacy was unfolding. Along with being inducted into the CIAA, I was chosen to be on the program as a speaker to represent the players from the '80s.

For those who were still in physical condition to play, we were invited to play in the Legends game. Whoever would have imagined that 16 years later, I would be given the opportunity to play again in front of the fans as a legend? Not only did my team win, but I also received another award for Top Rebounder.

Chapter 7
DREAMS DO COME TRUE

There was a dream that I would never relinquish. Unbelievably, decades later, this dream would come true. How committed are you to seeing your dreams manifest? What are you willing to give up, to sacrifice? How determined are you? I was very determined and as a result, hopefully my story will give you hope, strength and the courage to never give up on you!

I continued playing basketball for several professional teams between 1989 and 2000. During this period, I was successful in landing a position with the women's professional basketball team, the Philadelphia Rage, of the now defunct American Basketball League in 1996 (ABL). I was excited about the opportunity to get paid because the other professional teams that I had played for did not pay salaries. Depending on the team, some covered traveling costs, uniforms, and equipment in addition to giving stipends. They didn't have the notoriety and or funding compared to the ABL. Many of those leagues evidently folded due to financial reasons.

Now here was my chance to get paid and I refused to allow this opportunity to pass me by. Here is another example how my persistence paid off. I was determined to play for the ABL. So off I went. I called the main office and inquired about the process. I was advised to send them film, my player bio and any other pertinent information, stats, etc. for their review to determine if I would be invited to attend the combine. Upon review of my materials, they would inform me of their decision.

A few weeks later, I received a letter stating that although I had not been selected to attend the combine, I should contact each team individually. And so, I did. I sent all the same materials to all the 11 teams. I set up a daily schedule to contact and follow up with each team until I got results. There was "NO STOPPING ME NOW."

My conviction was strong. Robert and Vicki's mom was going to play professional basketball for the ABL. No matter how hard and challenging something may be, you have to persevere.

The closest team to me at that time was the Richmond Rage. During the middle of their season and right before I was to join the team, they moved to Philadelphia and renamed the team. They were now the Philadelphia Rage. Regardless, I was ready and prepared to go to Philadelphia, provided I made the team. Every call to their office, after the first call confirming that they had received my materials, was the same. "We are in the process of evaluating players and will get back to you soon. Our head coach, Lisa Boyer, makes all the decisions." This was good; now I had a name. I headed off to the Rage's office with a game plan in mind.

At the same time, I was being pursued by my alma mater for an assistant women's basketball coach position. It would be great if I landed both positions. I was living in the Maryland area and the drive to Richmond, Virginia was short of two hours. Before I headed down, I called and got permission to stop by the Rage office to introduce myself. Upon arriving to the office, I was greeted with a warm welcome from one of the staff members. I believe it was one of the assistant coaches.

Unfortunately, Coach Boyer had left the office for a meeting across town and they we not sure when she would be back. Nevertheless, I shared my intentions and my desire to try out for the team and provided updated statistics. We chatted for a few moments and before I left, she handed me two tickets to attend a home game. I was happy that I had gathered up enough nerve and courage to take this trip. Things were lining up for me.

I had a blast at the game. I got to meet a few of the players and the coaching staff, including Coach Boyer. I greeted her with my elevator speech and expressed an interest in trying out for her team. We chatted for a few minutes and then I left. I felt that I had made a connection and the next call attempt would hopefully grant me the opportunity to try out for the team.

A few weeks later, to my surprise, Coach Boyer answered the phone when I called. Just like I had envisioned and planned, my desire to obtain a tryout had now come true. She offered me the opportunity to join the team as a reserve and would evaluate me regularly for a roster spot.

She informed me that she couldn't promise me a position on the team. I told her that I understood and that I was not asking her to promise me a position, but only the opportunity to tryout. Because of the distance and my family situation, we agreed on a schedule that was mutually beneficial for the both of us. I would practice two to three times per week, which included one overnight stay. They would cover my travel expenses and food and allow me to stay with a couple of the players on the nights that I stayed back. I thanked her and hung up the phone.

With the news in hand, my family was excited. My children were ecstatic. Their mom is going to be a play professional basketball player. Here she goes again, they were astounded. I was eager to start, but nervous.

> I had made sacrifices in the past and they proved worthy.

Once again, my dream of playing professional basketball with the ABL was just around the corner. Could this really be happening or would I wake up and find it was all just a dream? Was I willing to drive back and forth to Philadelphia, a two-hour ride from Maryland, three to four days a week? What sacrifices would I have to make? Family, job, time to train?

My answer was absolutely, unequivocally, YES! I had made sacrifices in the past and they proved worthy. I was committed. I would make the journey. Nothing ventured, nothing gained.

I felt that my first day of practice went well. I was nervous and wondered what I had expected from myself and what would practice be like? Practicing and playing against elite players and who are now college and professional coaches, Dawn Staley, Taj McWilliams Franklin, Michelle Marciniak, Beth Morgan Cunningham, Adrienne Goodson, just to name few, was a breathtaking experience. Life was good! I demonstrated to the coaches and players that I had the skill and talent to effectively compete at the professional level.

Most of the players gave compliments and were surprised that at the age of 35, I was in great shape and at the prime of my game. Surprisingly, I felt that I was in better shape than a few of them. I competed every drill. I made the sprint times. I ran the floor and never missed a beat. When we stay true to our goals and do not waiver, great things can happen.

And then strife started at home, right before I was offered a roster position. The Director of Player Development from the front office of the ABL had approached me at one of our home games and told me that she had heard great things about my performance and would be in contact with me over the next couple of weeks. I was dealing with a significant amount of conflict and chaos at home. I would later be forced to decide between my family or basketball. I was devastated. What was I going to do? My marriage was in trouble. I was accused of not caring for my family. This wasn't true, but I was accused of only caring about basketball and myself.

Prior to my marriage and family, basketball had been my life. But after my family, I had always included them. They always came first. There was not a day when I didn't make sure everyone was taken care of. I was a wife, a mother, the PTA President and a chaperone. I volunteered in the community, coached my children's teams and had a professional career.

We kept them very involved and busy. We signed them up for just about every sport. There was soccer, basketball, football, volleyball and track and field, from little league all the way up through high school. They were involved with the Boys and Girls Club and the AAU (Athletic Amateur Union). I followed them all the way through college and Vicki through professional basketball. There was never a moment that I missed in supporting them with their academics and sports activities. Robert Jr. and Vicki were and will always be my pride and joy! Because of my strong commitment to my marriage and family, I quit the team.

This decision left a scar. I was distraught. Was this the end of my basketball career? Would I ever rebound and try it again? I made a vow to myself that if the opportunity presented itself again, I would, without hesitation, make a different decision. Years later, there would be another opportunity and a different decision. Down, but not out. I continued playing basketball with leagues in the area.

In 1997, at the inaugural of the WNBA, I tried out for Washington Mystics, Charlotte Sting and received an invitation from the Phoenix Mercury. I was excited about the opportunity to tryout for the Mercury because Cheryl Miller was the head coach at that time.

I felt that my chances would be better since I had come to know her on two other auspicious occasions. Our first encounter was when we were both inducted into the Communiplex Hall of Fame in 1986 and then I ran into her again at the 1987 Pan American tryouts. At the end of the tryout she shared with me that I had a good tryout. However, I did not make the team. She would keep my information on file for future reference.

I continued to play for several teams in the National Women's Basketball League. My experiences on different teams varied. The most memorable teams were the Maryland Sparks, Legacy and Booth All-Stars, all located in the Washington DC, Maryland area. We traveled all over the country. Our teams usually made it to the final four championship rounds and would have the honor of playing the games at universities located not far from where the WNBA Final Fours were being held. This arrangement presented me with more opportunities to play in front of the WNBA coaches and hopefully be recruited and offered a contract.

> **She was impressed with my stamina, defense and free throw shooting percentage**

A few years later, for some strange reason, I was encouraged to give it one more shot in making the WNBA roster; and preferably, the Washington Mystics, since it was in my area. I had been instrumental in developing a relationship with the Mystics coaches and organization at that time. My goal was to earn a spot on the roster as a player or as a coach.

Over the next few weeks, I was in constant contact with the interim head coach, Cathy Parsons. She and I had met and over time developed a professional relationship as head college coaches. She coached at Howard University and I coached at Prince George's Community College. She would often come to my games looking for players. Now, as the interim head coach of the Washington Mystics, she agreed to help me in any way that she could. I wanted an opportunity to tryout out for the Mystics. Because of our rapport, I might have a shot at trying out with the hope of making the team.

To allow Cathy to see me perform, I got her to agree to scrimmage my women's semi-professional team during the Mystics 1998 season. Our team was shocked. We were going to play against the Washington Mystics of the WNBA. They couldn't believe that I had pulled it off.

After the scrimmage, I spoke candidly with Cathy about my interest in becoming a member of the team. She told me that given her status, she was in no position to make any decision. The general manager did all the hiring for coaches and players. She recommended that I contact the GM and continue to work on my game. I contacted the GM. There were no openings.

My connection with the Washington Mystics organization developed as I continued pursing opportunities with them either as a player or coach despite the head coach changes over the next several years. In 2002, Washington Mystics hired Marianne Stanley as their new coach.

After getting the job, she sought to develop a professional relationship with the coaches in the Washington metropolitan area.

A few years earlier in 1999, I had accepted the women's basketball Head Coach position at Prince George's Community College in Largo, Maryland. She reached out to me and expressed an interest in coming out to our practices and games. She had heard about one of my players who had transferred and wanted to get to know more about the player and me. I was happy to know that a professional women's basketball team was interested in my player, a junior college player. Unfortunately, the player failed the next semester and her parents suggested that she quit college and come back home and work to help the family.

Over time, Coach Stanley and I developed a strong professional relationship. And then the unbelievable happened again. We ran into each other at a viewing of the 2002 WNBA Draft at the ESPN restaurant in DC. After a lengthy conversation and a phone call later with my trainer and I, she granted me an opportunity to participate in a closed tryout.

Here I come again. Whoop, I did it again! I was now 40 years of age and there was no letting up. Again, the news was not received well by my husband. As promised to myself earlier, I was not going to let this opportunity pass me by. He was just going to have to accept it. I was going to the tryout, with or without his support. Regardless of the outcome, I had already won. My name was on the list and I received preferential treatment as I entered the parking garage and arena. It was a dream come true.

At the tryouts, unbelievably, I was more in shape than many of the younger women. At the end of the tryouts, Coach Stanley was surprised that I had made it through the entire tryout. She was impressed with my stamina, defense and free throw shooting percentage. Months before the tryout, I had hired a personal trainer and worked out two to three times a day to prepare for this moment. I knew it was a long shot and I'm pretty sure that had I been younger, I would have made the team. How could she explain having a 40-year-old on her team in better shape than her younger players? This time I was not disappointed. Although I was humbled, I was proud of myself and would treasure this moment forever. It was and still is, well with my soul.

My ability to market myself was a skill that I had learned because of the many sales jobs I had and the training sessions that I was required to attend as a life insurance agent/investor for top financial companies in the Washington, DC metropolitan area.

As far as I can remember, I have always been a go-getter, self-motivated and determined. As mentioned many times throughout my book, I have this inexhaustible faith and regardless of the many challenges and adversities that come along with it, I have always, somehow found a way to push through.

My thirst for knowledge and being my best, while putting my best foot forward, is truly how I function. When we sit down to take a moment to quiet ourselves, we can discover the truth about our soul's mission. Many of us are too busy being busy and wondering why we either have not found our purpose and/or recognized our gift. It is in the quiet moments of more prayer, meditation and contemplation that the answers come.

I aspired to work with the Washington Mystics. This would be the culmination of all the success that I had achieved during my journey of becoming a standout professional basketball player. With the mindset that I could make it happen, with the same belief, hard work and determination that had become the cornerstone of my life, I put together a plan of action. I was an achiever. I knew that once I was clear about the process, I could manifest my goals.

A few years later in 2005, as I continued to coach at Prince George's Community College, I successfully fulfilled this goal. First, I submitted my cover letter and resume to the Mystics home office. Second, I made a trip down to their office to follow up. To my surprise, after a brief chat, they suggested that I make a trip over to one of the Mystic's practices and introduce myself to the coaching staff.

When they told me where they were practicing, I immediately knew that I would have a great chance of meeting the coaching staff. I was familiar with the college where they practiced and knew the women's basketball Head Coach very well. If need be, I would at least have her introduce me to Mystic's coaching staff and take it from there.

Finally, it happened. I got to meet Richie Adubato, who was the Head Coach for women's basketball for the Washington Mystics at that time. After our discussion, he offered me the opportunity to volunteer as a practice and scouting coach. I was elated. Through my faith and determination, I had done

it again. What I have come to realize and accept is that whatever we put our minds to and believe, along with the work we do, all things are possible. So be mindful of what you believe in. Be it positive or negative. Either way, your thoughts become reality. I am a living witness.

FROM PLAYER TO COACH

Barvenia Wooten-Collier '83, is the new head women's basketball coach at her alma mater.

A member of the 1983 Virginia Union National Championship team Wooten-Collier had previously coached at Prince George's (Maryland) Community College and was the 2005-06 Maryland JUCO Coach of the Year.

A four-year starter at Virginia Union, Wooten-Collier graduated in 1983 with a Bachelor's of Science Degree in Accounting. During her time at Virginia Union she was named an NCAA All-American. She is also a Virginia Union University Hall of Famer, and was inducted into CIAA Hall of Fame in 1999. She was a practice player for the ABL Philadelphia Rage.

Coach Wooten-Collier enjoys helping develop and enhance the skills of her women's basketball players as well as helping her young women become successful in their endeavors on and off the court.

1983 Women's National Championship Basketball Team

The two-year experience was priceless. The information that I learned would prove valuable and add greatly to my ability to effectively coach at all levels of basketball throughout my 19 years of coaching. I remain grateful and thankful to Coach Adubato for believing in me and giving me the opportunity to fulfill my goal.

I used the knowledge and coaching techniques I had gained from Coach Adubato to continue to build a winning and sustainable women's basketball culture and program at Prince George's Community College from 1999 through 2010. In my second year at PGCC, we won the 2001 Maryland Junior College Championship and I received Coach of the Year.

Five years later in 2006, we won our conference, regionals and advanced to the NJCAA National Women's Basketball Championship for the first time in the college's history. I was awarded the NJCAA District J Women's Division II Coach of the Year and we finished fifth in the nation. The last season of my tenure in 2010, we won again, advanced to the NJCAA National Women's Basketball Tournament and finished eleventh in the nation earning another Coach of the Year award. In addition to helping majority of my players earn athletic and/or academic scholarships to four-year institutions, I was successful in coaching two All-American players who were recruited to George Washington University & Virginia Commonwealth University on a full basketball scholarship.

Finally, I became Head Coach at my alma mater, Virginia Union University. After several discussions and meeting with VUU over a 19-year period, everything had come full circle. The spring before I started coaching in 2010, my jersey #31 would be retired as "The Greatest of Virginia Union University" and currently hangs in the rafters. During my five years there, I turned the program around and helped prepare for its success to come after I left. In my second year there, we won the 2012 Northern Division of our conference and I was named Coach of the Year. This would be my fifth time receiving this honor, four of them during my tenure at PGCC.

An interesting thing that also happened during this journey while coaching at VUU is that I was fortunate to have my daughter, Vicki Collier as a coach and a player.

I offered her the opportunity to be my assistant coach during my first year at Virginia Union University. I thought this would be a great experience for both of us. Here we were, mother and daughter, coaching at my alma mater, which would soon turn out to be hers as well. A mother and daughter coaching team were certainly rare. We were the first to coach together at Virginia Union and in our basketball conference, the CIAA.

I believe our record still stands to this day for both organizations. We would appear in Women's Basketball Coaching Association magazine, Coaching Women's Basketball Mid-Season Issue 2011, with the legendary Coach, Geno Auriemma. The article, "Like Mother, Like Daughter," discussed how our relationship transitioned into "Coach and Coach" and how we made the adjustments now as professionals at the collegiate level.

It was truly an honor that had come full circle for the both of us as we ended the first year's season. The following season with Vicki would be the most rewarding. She would transition from assistant coach to player. "Mother is Her Coach and Daughter is Her Star," read the Richmond Free Press.

VUU standout Vicki Collier happily poses with her mother and basketball coach, Barnia Wooten-Cherry, who led the Lady Panthers to a national hoops title in 1983. Together, they're trying to return the VUU women's program to powerhouse status.

This would be the first of many articles and awards to come during that season. Vicki would help us to capture the 2012 CIAA Northern Division Championship. Just like her mom decades later, she too would be named Player of the Week and lead the 2012 All Conference CIAA Team.

Many people have often asked me what it was like to coach my daughter. My experience was both challenging and rewarding, sort of paradoxically. But overall, the experience was great. How many people get a chance to have their children coach with them at the collegiate level, as well as play for them? Not many and especially at their alma mater.

Like Mother, Like Daughter

by Vicki Friedman

Vicki Collier can't always keep it straight. What exactly should she be calling her mother these days? At the office she'll start with "mom" and catch herself. Oops. I mean coach, coach."

In the townhouse they share, she has to stop herself again. "Coach ... I mean mom," Barvenia Wooten-Collier has it easier. Daughter Vicki is simply "Coach V" around the office they share at Virginia Union University. At home, she's Vicki.

Barvenia (R) and Vicki (L) address their team in the hud during a recent gar
VIRGINA UNION ATHLETI

Lady Panthers Win First Divisional Title in Nine Years

It was a blessing and an honor to have both children work with me as an assistant coach and later, have Vicki play for me at the collegiate level. Robert Jr. was the first to coach with me as my assistant coach at my first head coaching position at Prince George's Community College during the 2005 season.

Vicki came along years later in 2010 as my first assistant coach at our alma mater, Virginia Union University. Then, after playing for me the 2011–12 season, she would rejoin my coaching staff until my departure in 2015. I will always cherish these moments, as they will always be memorable events of my life. It seems like yesterday when I was tending to their every move and desire. Motherhood was very special to me. I had looked forward to having children as a child.

Initially, I wanted eight children. This desire came from my childhood experience with two of my best girlfriends who came from large families of at least 17. I thought it was cool having a lot of siblings to help with doing chores and always having someone to play with and talk to.

This desire would immediately change after giving birth to my first child,

Robert Jr. The pregnancy process was good up to the delivery! I couldn't imagine having to go through that seven more times. Two times would be enough. Then, after the birth of Vicki, that sealed the deal. Eight became three and three now became two. I was satisfied with having my two children, a boy and a girl.

It was my goal to be very involved in the growth and development of my children. I wanted to give them a stable and loving home. I wanted them to succeed at whatever they would decide to do. Early on in their lives I began to plant positive seeds in their minds about their God-given talents and abilities and that they could accomplish any and everything that they put their minds to. My goal was to make sure that no matter what the challenges or circumstances, they both would be well educated and knowledgeable.

As I have mentioned, I believe in the message, "A mind is a terrible thing to waste." And I, within all my power, was determined to make sure they didn't. And I did. Both children would attend a public school for the gifted during their formative years and both would finish at private schools.

Robert's first two years were at DeMatha Catholic High School and his last two years were at Riverdale Baptist. Vicki's three years were at Largo High School and her last year, ironically, was at Riverdale Baptist. Both would graduate as scholar athletes.

Robert and Vicki are four years apart. It was great having them graduate and finish strong from the same high school. Their graduations were a wonderful experience. Unlike public school graduations with literally thousands of people, their graduations were personal and sacred. I truly appreciated the celebrations and closeness that I felt from the school and the pastor. There was a spiritual overtone that I experienced and enjoyed immensely. I was ecstatic and happy for them.

Not only had they been exposed to the principles of the sacredness of their growth and experience at the Unity church we had been attending, they were now being given a second dose of the covering of God from their schooling at Riverdale. The ceremonies were special and memorable.

During the last three years as Head Coach at VUU, the recognition continued. In 2013, I was awarded VUU Presidential Citation Award and inducted into the Cincinnati Public Schools Athletic Hall of Fame, the first athlete from my high school, Hughes High School and the entire City of Cincinnati.

That same year, the NCAA would fly me out to San Diego, California to name and honor me as a member of the NCAA Division II 40th Anniversary Tribute Team to commensurate and recognize the rich history of student-athletes at the Division II institutions who have flourished both in athletics competition and as citizen-leaders beyond their playing days. This award ceremony was very special to me. I was able to celebrate with 39 other outstanding student-athletes from all over the country who also would leave a legacy of greatness for others, including their children, to remember and hopefully follow in their footsteps.

Then in 2014, I was selected to attend the NCAA Women Coaches Academy, Alliance of Women Coaches, to be held in Atlanta, Georgia, for a week of training. This experience would expose me to other women who coached different sports at different levels from around the world. The training program was well structured. The instructors were very knowledgeable about their individual subject matter. The information and materials were presented in an organized and concise manner.

We were challenged every day to study the materials presented the day before and engage in the daily discussions by sharing our own individual experiences and knowledge with the class. Our day began at 6:00 AM and usually ended by 7:00 PM, with a few breaks and lunch in between.

We were encouraged to build and develop professional relationships with each other in class and after class at the scheduled networking events. Our days were long and exhausting, yet the knowledge and experience was gratifying. I learned what it truly meant to be a "professional" in my career.

Not everyone can be a coach. The long hours, the commitment and dedication are a must to be successful and fulfilling and there is the sacrifice of time and family. I was determined like always to finish strong. The regime that I was exposed to during this training benefitted me greatly.

Even as an author, I used the techniques and methods that I learned while a student at the Coaches Academy to help me get through this writing process. When it was all said and done, I finished as a "Professional Women's Basketball Coach."

In 2015, with four years of success behind me, the last year as a professional coach at VUU would present unforeseeable challenges on the court. It was a rollercoaster year for me as we were plagued by injuries and some internal conflicts. After meeting with the new athlete director at the end of the season, I decided to resign.

As I reflected on my tenure with VUU, I was able to revitalize the women's basketball program and prepare it for the success to come later. We had become known as one of the best and talented teams, advancing to the semifinal rounds during the CIAA tournaments, beating teams sometimes by as much as 30 points or more.

McDonald's Restaurants
SALUTE
THE 1986 COMMUNIPLEX WOMEN'S SPORTS HALL OF FAME INDUCTEES FOR THEIR CONTRIBUTION TO WOMEN'S ATHLETICS

=== NATIONAL ===

Barvenia Wooten Collier
Basketball
Virginia Union University

Jody Conradt
Basketball
University of Texas

A Special Tribute to
Mildred "Babe" Didrickson Zaharias
(deceased)
Golf and Track
Olympian

Debbie Green
Volleyball
Olympian

Flo Hyman (Deceased)
Volleyball
Olympian

Jenny Johnson
Softball
Franklin University

Kathy Johnson
Gymnastic
Olympian

Cheryl Miller
Basketball
University of Southern California

Diana Nyad
Swimming (Long Distance)
Network Sports Commentator

=== LOCAL ===

Linda Norwell
Basketball
University of Cincinnati

Sharon Moore
Volleyball
Finneytown High School

Tom Louis
Basketball
Seton High School

Mary Jo Huismann
Basketball
Mother of Mercy High School

Cindy Crilley
Tennis
Indian Hills High School
Indiana University

Mary Jett Ritter
Volleyball
Seton High School

HALL OF FAME INDUCTION CEREMONY TO BE HELD AT OMNI NETHERLAND HALL OF MIRRORS AT 11:30 a.m. FRIDAY, NOVEMBER 28, 1986

Mae Faggs Starr
Track (Olympian)
Princeton High School

UP & RUNNING 137

I coached several ALL CIAA Conference players, including Ashle Freeman, who would surpass me as the number two scoring leader in the history of women's basketball at VUU; Lady Walker, who would go on to become the 2016 CIAA Defensive and Player of the Year; and Taylor Smith, 2016 CIAA Scholar Athlete of the Year.

It was truly a blessing to know that all the players that I had recruited and who had played at VUU during their entire four years under my leadership, graduated. Some have gone on to become either assistant or head coaches at the high school and/or collegiate levels. Although my contract ended, I left behind a strong legacy and an indelible mark as a coach and a player.

After taking a year off from coaching, I decided to return home to Cincinnati to help with my aging mom. During this time, I landed a job with USJN (United States Junior National) BlueStar Media as an Evaluator. This position allowed me to attend all the area girls' basketball showcases sponsored by USJN and evaluate the talent levels of the players. It was fun and exciting. It was no different than when I was a coach out recruiting. The process was the same. The only difference was that I didn't have an invested interest in the players since I was not personally recruiting.

Through this experience, I was able to network with other evaluators and meet coaches from all levels and from across the country, building professional and long-lasting relationships. I was also able to reconnect with the group of coaches that I already had a rapport and/or relationship established.

While this position only lasted for a short period of time, my recruiting skills increased greatly. As time went on, I realized how much I missed coaching. So, I decided to hit the trail again applying for coaching jobs.

After approximately 40 or more applications, unlimited phone calls and several interviews either over the phone or face-to-face, I was hired as the Head Coach at Florida State College at Jacksonville (FSCJ) in August 2016, where I stayed until my separation in June 2019 to travel back home again to help care for my elderly mother.

Over the span of three years, I successfully trained, prepared and helped all my sophomores get recruited on full scholarships to play at the four-year level and every player I recruited remained with me their two years and graduated. Everywhere that I have coached, my philosophy included making sure my student-athletes graduated and this mindset had began my signature.

Because of my dedication and commitment to the women's basketball program, the athletic department and the community, we were the first recipients of the 2016–17 Life Skills Award started by the Athletic Director my first year at FSCJ. The following year, FSCJ Administrative & Professional Collaborative (APC), the representative voice for the Administrative & Professional employees, honored me with the December 2018 Spotlight Award for my service to the college.

As I think back over my coaching career thus far, I recognize a pattern that is very insightful. No matter the wins and losses, the graduation rates, championships, individual and team awards or accomplishments, I have left a legacy of helping others. As I started my career path in coaching over 30 years ago, I made a commitment to myself that graduating my student-athletes would be equally important as winning championships. This was a feat that I didn't take lightly.

Chapter 8
A SPIRITUAL AWAKENING & REVELATION

Over the span of my life, church has played a very important part in the development of my spiritual walk. We had been raised in the church. With my mother being an ordained minister, there was no escaping going to church. We were taught to pray every day and assured that God, the Divine, would answer our prayers.

Singing in the choirs, ushering and taking on leadership roles helped develop my character and my love to help others. I had even considered becoming a minister just like my mom. I always enjoyed listening when my mother preached.

She had a powerful voice and spoke passionately on every subject. She was fierce, and in her mid-80s, is still equally fierce. She doesn't back down from anyone. I mean that literally and figuratively. I believe that trait was passed on to my late brother, Alan and me. Although we both took on this trait, in the life of my brother, his would be much more brash than mine.

He too, didn't back down from anyone. Unfortunately, this mindset might possibly have led to his untimely passing. My ability to speak my voice was directed in a way to stand up for myself and for others against injustices. I believe that everyone has rights and should be treated as human beings regardless of the color of their skin, race, ethnicity, etc. I assumed everyone thought this way. However, I find, from time to time, that this is not always the mindset of others.

> **I had developed a passion for getting closer to God, the Divine.**

Over the years, I have been a part of several different churches, always looking for the best fit for my spiritual growth and later on for my family. At every church, I either sang in the choir and/or ushered. I always believed in participating and joining different ministries. This was my way of giving back and working for God.

After having my children, I continued my search for a church home to fulfill my spiritual needs. One day, a co-worker introduced me to her church, the Unity Center of Light. During a brief conversation, she shared with me the great things that were being taught at Unity about spirituality. This idea of spirituality intrigued me. She invited me and my family to be her guest the following Sunday. After the first time we attended Unity, my children and I were hooked.

At Unity, like some other churches, they provided classes for children under 17 during church services. I liked this idea. At the end of service, my children expressed how much fun they had and all the activities that they did. We were sold. If the children liked it that much, then this was, again, another confirmation of being in alignment.

Unity would transform my beliefs about my existence, my thoughts about religion and how I viewed God for the rest of my life. I had no idea just how much my spiritual life would change. The reawakening of my soul had begun and I would be in for a great surprise as I searched for the true meaning of my existence and my understanding of God and its relationship to the universe.

Over the next several weeks, I attended every event, meeting and activity that they had to learn more about Unity. I was hungry and thirsty for gaining more knowledge and understanding about my relationship with this being called God.

The lessons given by the pastor were deep and initially beyond my comprehension and understanding, although they were Bible-based. The messages challenged us to take a real deep look within ourselves to find our own connection with divinity and why we exist. We were encouraged to commit to developing strong study habits and to set aside periods of daily prayer and meditation. We were taught that the power within ourselves is greater than anything outside of ourselves and that this power within is our source, God.

Just like before, I had made a commitment to read and study the Bible. It was my goal to read the Bible in its entirety along with other spiritual books and materials. Although, I haven't accomplished the goal of reading the entire Bible yet, my understanding of the difference between religion, spirituality and consciousness took on a whole new meaning.

I began to understand that the Scriptures that I learned from my earlier upbringing had played an important role in how I functioned and made it through most of life's adversities.

Further contemplation of the Scriptures increased my knowledge and broadened my perspective and outlook on life. I had developed a passion for getting closer to God, the Divine. The wonderful thing that happened during my quest to know God on a deeper level was the spiritual growth of my children.

They too were heavily involved in most of the children's activities.

They attended many of the retreats for children. They held many roles during youth day services, they made presentations and lead group discussions within their respective groups.

Unity Center of Life would serve as the spiritual foundation for Robert and Vicki too. Robert was twelve and Vicki was eight when we joined Unity and continued attending Unity throughout most of their collegiate years. As the Vice-President of her group, the Uni-Teens, Vicki would be the only member of our family to get the opportunity to travel and visit the headquarters of Unity in Kansas City, Missouri for a week.

I believe that this experience had a profound effect on the development of Vicki's philosophy on life and opened her desire to explore her own beliefs about God. I believe that my family was destined to find Unity. The principles and doctrines that we were introduced to shaped and molded us while providing us with a strong spiritual foundation to build upon.

I know that deep down inside of my children and me, there is a spiritual connection that resonates between us. I feel confident that our souls will remain with each other for an eternity.

My faith has gotten stronger because of my commitment to this process of learning more about how I see and understand who God truly is to me. I have come to an understanding that God cannot be defined. God is in every one of us and is everywhere present. The moment we attempt to define God, we limited his omnipresent power. The universe is massive and there are no boundaries.

As I took on this new mindset, I began to see how important it was to embrace all religions and that no one religion is superior to another. Everyone has their individual perception of God. For me, when I speak of God throughout my book, I refer to God as Spirit, Divine Intelligence.

I have come to accept that everyone has a responsibility to develop their own personal relationship with their belief as to who God is to them and that we should not judge them for their choice. We were all given freewill to worship based on our individual and personal beliefs. Therefore, I believe that we are accountable for our everyday decisions and actions and cannot blame any one person, thing or deity.

Every day is a test. We are all presented with our own individual challenges and sometimes we perceive that we are the only ones with problems. Like so many others and many times in my life, my faith would be tested like never before. Like many relationships and marriages, I too had my share of disappointments and challenges. There were good times and bad times.

I believed in the holy sanctity of marriage and never dreamed of or believed in divorce. And then it happened. The union that I had believed in and fought for was now ending. Twenty-five years later, married for twenty-one, with two beautiful children, my life would take on a different path. How could this be? I asked myself over and over if I should keep fighting for it, be patient and seek the Divine for answers. What are people going to say? What about my family and friends? Most importantly, what about our children? How do I tell my mother? Did I have the strength and courage to endure? This would be one of the most challenging times in my life. My faith was certainly being tested.

However, because of the commitment that I had made earlier to my spiritual work, I found the strength and courage that I didn't know I had as I continued to trust God, the Divine. It was truly by grace, prayer and one of my best girlfriends, Mavis Turner, I got through the process of divorce.

After much contemplation and soul searching, as crazy as it sounds, this was the turning point of my spiritual walk, my journey with God, the Divine. Little did I know, I was being re-birthed. Just like before with my other religious experiences, most of my time was spent at the Unity Center of Light seeking answers for guidance and direction. Self-actualization was happening. I was finding myself all over again.

At first, I found myself questioning my existence and blaming myself for the divorce. How could this be happening to me, to us? Up to this point in my life, I didn't believe in divorce. I believed that if I was not being physically abused, then I needed to do everything I could, including counseling, to save my marriage. But over time, things just got worse. It was time to let go and allow myself to heal and cleanse.

Once I let go and got very clear about how I planned to move forward, everything seemed to fall right in place, even amidst all the turmoil, grief, pain and agony that I went through. After a 25-year relationship, how could two people walk away and call it quits? I've never been a quitter. However, this time it was beyond my control. He wanted out. And for some strange reason, I did too.

Let me say for the record, this is not about who was right and who was wrong. It's about my transitioning into another chapter of my life by overcoming what seemed impossible to overcome. For some, divorce can leave a lifetime of such emotional and psychological scars as bitterness, resentment, abandonment, embarrassment, hatred, unforgiveness and even possible suicide.

Like always, I was determined to find a way to heal and move forward. Here come my angels again. Right on time. Now a member of the Unity Center of Light, a non-denominational spirituality center, my quest to learn the truth about my existence, the world, the universe and God began to present itself.

As a result, three very important people, my angels, showed up affirming that the time was now to transform and that I was at the right place, right time and mindset to prepare me for the new chapter and new path that awaited me. The first angel was the minister of the center. His appearance into my life was to help and guide me through my spiritual awakening.

As mentioned earlier, the lessons that he presented on Sundays and sometimes during the week were very profound, engaging and intriguing. I like the notion that we, as members, were challenged to seek the truth for ourselves and that we shouldn't rely on anyone else's opinion, knowledge or beliefs about what they thought or how they viewed their own existence and who God was to them.

We were encouraged to seek answers to our questions about God through daily prayers, meditations and reading and studying, not only the Bible, but also other recommended spiritual materials. I found myself drawn more and more to this new process. It resonated with my soul. This process allowed me to take my focus off my situation and focus on me and how imperative it was for me to let go and let God.

I began to come to the realization that I had to first forgive myself before I could forgive my husband so that my healing could begin. Another angel, Oni Afryae, fulfilled my need to cleanse physically and emotionally. A dear friend of ours had referred Oni to me, because as I was going through transformation. I had decided to cut my permed hair and go natural.

> **Like always, I was determined to find a way to heal and move forward.**

This was a symbolic sign of the beginning of my physical cleanse. When we met initially, we thought it was about my hair and for her to become my hairstylist. She was a lock technician and had come highly recommend as I began this phase. We soon realized that although going natural was a great way to transition, it was just the catalyst that brought us together for a greater purpose.

Her purpose for coming into my life at that appointed time was threefold. A few appointments later, we discovered that she was a divine appointment. She was very knowledgeable on various subjects and topics about methods recommended to help women interested in cleansing their physical bodies for spiritual and holistic reasons. The goal was to rid themselves of toxins that had built up over the course of one's life that had been or were detrimental to their health and well-being.

Again, I was all in. I was hooked. This was a definite confirmation that I was on the right path and headed in the right direction. I felt very good and excited about this change. I embraced it with every fiber of my being.

The time had come and I was prepared. Oni and I were both enthused about the process. She would be my teacher and advisor and I would be her student and in some cases, her study. After explaining to me her position on natural hair and about the potential harmful effects of dying and perming my hair, I made a conscientious decision that I would not go back to perming my hair.

This has been my own personal choice and decision for me. In no way am I claiming that there are negative effects of using chemicals on hair. However, it has been documented and confirmed that the chemicals used to process and straighten out Africa-American course hair could very well be toxic and damaging to the strength and health of hair and potentially affect the scalp. Further research and other reliable sources revealed that the constant application of the chemicals could also potentially affect brain cells. This was enough information to help me make an informed decision that I felt was in my best interest.

And then came the physical cleansing of changing my diet and partaking in a holistic six-week total body cleansing session that would require much discipline and sacrifice of my time and resources. I was all in, body, soul and spirit. This was truly the start of the awakening of my soul. The cleansing process began with information and classes on choosing to become a vegetarian or a vegan.

After watching videos on how animals were being slaughtered and how, on many occasions, some of the sick animals were slaughtered along with the healthy animals, for some strange reason I could feel their pain as they went through the slaughter process. No animal should be treated this way, as there were many acts of inhumane treatment.

The knowledge that I received about the importance of how we should love and treat all living creatures was enlightening. As a result, I went cold-turkey (no pun intended!) and stopped eating beef and pork immediately. It was maybe a year or two later that I gave up poultry. I no longer was to be a part of eating animals and the flesh of any other creatures. Meat would no longer be a part of my diet. My family was shocked. They could not understand how I could just stop eating meat after 35 years of it being an essential part of my diet. But I was sold.

As this process was unfolding, I began the total body cleansing sessions. It was recommended that I do both processes at the same time. That would involve removing meat from my diet along with starting the cleansing program. It would prove to be beneficial to my health and well-being over the next several years.

I had fallen in love with animals, a love that I had never experienced. Eating them was out of the picture. I have remained committed to my vegetarian diet with hopes of going vegan. Everyone's growth or transformation process is different and while this dietary change works for me, it might not work for others. I began incorporating a plant based diet.

The people at the sessions that I attended were very encouraging and helpful. They had their own plant food restaurant and as often as I could afford it, I ate there. The food was simply amazing. They also taught us how to prepare and cook vegetarian dishes. Interestingly, the preparation and cook time was way less than cooking with meat.

As I was learning about the plant diet and being educated on the different kinds of herbs and spices, I began to experience this connection with nature. It was unexpected, yet very inviting. I could feel the transformation taking place within me. I knew I was on the right path and this was my destiny. My life had taken on a new meaning and and it was exhilarating and refreshing.

As I prepared for the total body cleansing sessions, I incorporated some of the lessons that I had learned during the dietary sessions. They seemed to work hand in hand. Everything collaborated and flowed with ease.

I believe that when you have these types of epiphanies, aha moments, you are in alignment with your soul's mission. I was in alignment. Oni introduced me to a six-week program designed by Queen Afua, a holistic health practitioner and wellness coach, who wrote a book called, Sacred Women: A Guide to Healing the Female Mind, Body and Spirit.

This took me through a series of Afrocentric spiritual practices that required a commitment to rising as early as 4:00 AM in the morning and preparing for bed by sunset. Again, I was open, ready and willing to go through this process. It was as if my soul was crying out. I needed this sacred healing. It was time. The process was challenging, but well worth the investment.

Although Oni was involved in another healing program, she supported and encouraged me throughout the entire time. We were required to cleanse our kitchen of all processed products, including white flours, sugars and products made with bleached flour, breads, pasta and canned foods. Our kitchens were to be our sacred laboratory because that is where our health and wealth live.

> The moment we attempt to define God, we limited his omnipresent power.

I recall one weekend when my daughter was home for the weekend from college. As she looked in the pantry and cabinets, they were practically empty. She was shocked and surprised as she said, "Mom, where are the snacks, the cookies and chips? The only thing that you have in the cabinets is falafel and couscous and there is only lettuce and spinach in the refrigerator."

She and I laughed and laughed. She decided to play a joke on her father and called him, pretending to be crying and told him that I didn't have any food in the house for her. Initially, he thought that she was crying for real and told her that he was going to call Social Services on me. I replied, in a joking manner as well, that I was going to call the Department of Health on him because all he had in his refrigerator were dead animals. We all laughed, as this was truly a memorable event and moment.

As we continued with the programs, Oni and I developed a strong sisterhood and a bond that will never be broken as long as we are on this planet together. And let me just mention before I move on to my next angel, she has a beautiful son, Selah, who was just an infant when we met and agreed to work together on our spiritual healing.

We both believed he helped us along our journey as transformation was taking place. As a newborn, his presence symbolized, at least for me, that I was being reborn and that this course of action was on purpose. I developed a strong bond with him as well.

At the end of the six-week process, I felt renewed. I had reached another milestone in my life that would strengthen my inner being and illuminate my spirit. This process had taught me how important it was to take time to cleanse from within and allow the body to heal naturally. The results spoke for themselves.

I gained a deeper understanding on how to love myself from an inherent level, which helped me to heal from the emotional scars of my divorce and move forward. I had given so much of myself to my family, friends, helping others and my career. Here was an opportunity to focus on me. Unconsciously, I needed to be rejuvenated.

I felt lighter and more vibrant. I experienced from a deeper level what cleansing was about. My health improved. I lost unwanted fat. My skin had a glow. I was in the best physical shape of my life. Family and friends complimented me on how well I looked and that there was something different about me. And there was.

In addition to the internal changes, there was a spiritual change. My soul rejoiced. I had committed to a new lifestyle that proved valuable to my overall well-being. I was willing to truly forgive myself for any bad choices or decisions that I thought I had made. I had to accept full responsibility for my choices and actions. There was no one to blame.

I believe this is truly the moment when I acknowledged the belief that the power within me is far greater than any power outside of me and that no one or thing has power over me, my life or affairs. I remain thankful and grateful for taking the time to go through this process and be obedient to my soul's request. This revelation of learning to love myself unconditionally opened a bountiful blessing for me.

Who is this person, this tall, slim and good-looking man commanding my attention as he chatted with other members of our Center in our Fellowship Hall? It was Godfrey Cherry, who would later become my second husband. His voice was reassuring and he spoke with confidence as he shared his knowledge and understanding about his belief of who God was to him.

His conversation intrigued me. I wanted to learn more of his perspective. I quickly introduced myself. The moment we shook hands and made eye contact, I experienced a spiritual connection. It was as if the hands of time turned back and I was sixteen again.

I shared with him my spiritual knowledge and that I wanted to introduce him to one of the many books that I was reading, the 30-Day Mental Diet. This book encouraged its readers to commit to a 30-day process of thinking positive thoughts. Its purpose was to help one control the negative thoughts that randomly appear in our minds every waking moment.

For each of the 30 days, there was a positive message followed by a quote and Scripture requiring the reader to recite it three times a day. You were required to make a journal entry recording the results of the experience that the message had on you by the end of the day. I ran to the car to get the book, like a little child excited to show off my toy for show and tell. What an incredible moment.

Over the next few months, we would meet at Starbucks and Barnes & Noble, spending countless hours reading together on all topics involving spiritual growth and personal development. My soul was on a quest for truth and it was evident by the events that were occurring in my life.

In addition to the reading, we started to hang out together, going to the park, playing basketball, taking long drives, visiting places that I had always wanted to visit, museums, attending poetry night events and mostly, riding our bikes. Many nights we would sit at Reagan National Airport, watching the airplanes as they flew over us either taking off or landing. I enjoyed just being still.

His presence in my life was another divine appointment. We were destined to meet each other. The moment was right. The stars in the universe had lined up and answered my call to experience a demonstration of unconditional love for my soul. Godfrey's willingness to be a part of my journey, sacrificing his time and resources, was not for his own personal gain. His actions affirmed for me the meaning of unconditional love.

He too taught me how to love myself based on his unselfishness and kindness. I fell in love with myself all over again and it felt good. Although we divorced three years after our marriage, he and I have remained close and the bond that we built will last throughout eternity. Our relationship was and has been, all about our co-existence with the Divine and for spiritual growth.

They say things good or bad come in threes. For me, these three individuals, whom I refer to as my angels, came into my life at the right moments and the right times. My soul yearned for this healing. It was time to awaken to the next chapter of my life and I needed to go through this transition to move forward. Each of these individuals represented a significant part in my spiritual development, the healing of my soul and awakening me to Divine love.

My minister, Reverend Butch's teachings opened the door to my mind to explore the truth of my being, my purpose and reason for existence. Then, Oni came along and provided me with the information and resources necessary to cleanse my body through a series of spiritual methods and changing my diet for the purification of my body. And, finally, Godfrey, which was so apropos, showed me through his unselfish actions what unconditional love was. I had come to love and value myself once again. My soul had awakened!

Unlike before, I was adamant about getting a clear prospective about my relationship with God, the Divine. I would focus on living my life for Spirit, the Divine. I have come to accept that I am a vessel through which God operates and in which I move and have my being. The journey of my life thus far has been enlightened and expanded as I have evolved. I have learned so much about myself throughout this spiritual process.

The most profound thing that I realized about myself was whenever I became clear about what I wanted to accomplish and achieve, I was able to manifest it. This realization aligns with my belief that we have the power to create whatever we want and affirms that we will be given the desires of our heart if we are clear and believe. Be clear and believe!

Chapter 9
THE JOURNEY CONTINUES

My next move! So, what's next for Barvenia? As you can see, my life has revolved around sports. As I continue to allow my life to unfold and continue this journey, I remain excited and committed to adding to my legacy.

What I have come to know is that all of us were born with gifts and talents and it's up to us to seek and find them. Some people find and recognize them early, while others are still searching. I am excited and enthused that I have started my own professional women's basketball team, The Richmond Road Runners of the newly formed Women's Professional Basketball Association (WPBA). As a published author, business owner and up and coming international speaker, the journey continues as my life unfolds chapter by chapter.

I'm always checking in with myself during prayers, meditations and everyday thinking, asking, "Why am I here?" "How can I be the best highest version of myself?" "How can I continue reaching as many people as I can to help them discover their true essence?" I believe strongly in my ability to inspire others to pursue their dreams.

Many have encouraged me to consider speaking tours to share my stories and wisdom with others, mainly with the youth. To which I agree. The notion that we where all born to awaken to our gifts and talents and use them to help and share them with others drives me to work everyday at being the highest version of myself. I'm excited about these new opportunities and paths that await me. In addition to owning and coaching my professional women's basketball team, it's time to embrace my other gifts and talents, author and international inspirational speaker.

As far as I can remember, writing and speaking were talents that, although developed over time, I believe are my natural gifts. They needed to be developed and refined. And they were. All my careers have required me to write and speak on a large scale.

My first public speaking opportunity presented itself in high school. I was so nervous that I fumbled and was ashamed of the outcome. I felt invisible, as if no one heard me as I spoke. My words seemed to get lost somewhere between my voice and the audience's ears. I felt the same kind of fear that Ralph Ellison, the author of the Invisible Man, experienced in a scene when he too had to speak up about the fear of his existence. As he spoke, there was a void, a disconnect of his words, between himself and the listeners and thus, he felt invisible as a black man living in what he perceived, at that time, to be a white world oblivious to the black race. The next time I spoke I would be ready. I didn't want to relive the same feeling and outcome.

I decided to get help with speaking. The difficulty that I experienced the first time I spoke was not going to defeat me. I'm a winner and I wanted to succeed at everything I did. I asked around the school to see who could possibly help teach and train me. Later, I would receive coaching from one of the administrators at my high school. He instructed me to find a spot on the wall at the back of the room and focus my attention on that area as I spoke and to initially avoid eye contact with my audience until I had developed the confidence in my ability to speak without being fearful.

Over time, I became more confident in my ability to speak to large groups.

I had occasionally experienced butterflies when I hadn't prepared myself. My college experiences in many leadership positions provided me the platforms to build on my speaking capabilities. This increased my confidence and my abilities to speak in a clear and concise manner, sometimes even without a written message.

As captain of our high school and college basketball teams, treasurer of my chapter's sorority, Ms. Sophomore and Miss Virginia Union University, these leadership positions required me to speak regularly, enhancing my oral and written communication skills.

As I moved on with various careers, I often found myself having to speak, mostly as a basketball coach and financial planner. On many occasions, I was invited to be a guest speaker for several major organizations, including my alma mater, Virginia Union University. I was asked to be their guest speaker at the 2003 Athletic Banquet. What an honor!

I would never have imagined that decades later I would be invited back to speak and seven years later return as Head Coach. My desire to be known for motivating and empowering others had materialized. On two other most auspicious occasions, I was invited as guest speaker for two different basketball officiating organizations. One was with the Maryland Officiating Board 34, Largo, MD. Over several years, I had developed a professional relationship with this organization as a recognized coach for several youth basketball groups. The other was for the Central Intercollegiate Athletic Association (CIAA). I was ecstatic.

I was player and coach under the CIAA and now a guest speaker.

> My desire to be known for motivating and empowering others had materialized.

Amazing. It was a great experience. Both groups complimented me on how well I spoke and that they would keep me on file for future opportunities. My other speaking engagements included youth sports organizations' events, high school banquets and churches.

I have always enjoyed the opportunity to share with others, either through my words or my deeds. I believe that no one came here to fail. Why would we be here? There must be a reason and a purpose. We all have a destiny to fulfill. Some will and some won't.

Those who are self-disciplined, have a greater chance of succeeding. Self-discipline has been and will remain, the key to my success, which allowed me to create and establish standards that have kept me focused on achieving my goals and aspirations.

As I write this book, I see how writing and speaking came naturally to me and how much I looked forward to speaking and the joy that I received. I realized that I was intrigued by the thought of public speaking. I felt compelled to share with others the greatness that lives within each of us.

As mentioned throughout this book, I wanted everyone who I encountered, especially our youth, to believe in themselves and their ability to achieve their goals and dreams. I can imagine how powerful and inspiring it would be to help others recognize the gifts and talents that exist within them, knowing that they too can live meaningful and purposeful lives.

Life is what we make it. It's about the decisions that we make each minute, hour and every day. We must be cognizant that when we choose not to make decisions, life will make them for us. The ramifications that come from not making a decision are very impactful. When I find myself struggling with making the right decision. I refer to a technique that was taught to me by one of my mentors. He advised me to weigh the pros and cons. Make the decision and move forward. Don't look back or second-guess myself. Make it work. There is not a right or wrong decision. It is when we don't make a decision at all that we fail.

I have come to understand that we must create good habits, become self-disciplined and relentlessly work strategically to achieve our goals. We must develop a hunger and diligently pursue the meaning and purpose of our reason for being. For me, I believe that I found a path in sports and education at a young age. It was clear. As I have evolved, I have discovered other gifts and talents that I possess. And now, as I continue this journey, I realize that we all have several gifts and talents. Some we find early and some we discover later. Nevertheless, they all should fulfill our desires.

I have heard and have read hundreds of times that we should pursue that which we have a passion for and not just a job or career because of the money and prestige. Follow your passion and the money will follow. It might require a lot of sacrifice of time and resources, but at the end, you will find happiness. You will, as I have, find that which makes your heart sing with joy. You can't buy happiness and you can't place a price on it, because happiness comes from inside. Many times, we all rely on external things, people, places and stimulants to make us happy. They are all temporary and fleeting. Trust in yourself and know that you are worthy of everything that your heart yearns for and desires.

What if you woke up one day and realized that you were living your life to please others and now you find yourself working in a job or career that doesn't bring you joy and happiness. Every day you regret going to that job or being in that career. If you are not in the job or career that fulfills you, are you willing to make the change? Are you willing to make the sacrifice of your time and resources? It's never too late to change your mindset. By doing so, you can position yourself to move in the direction that ignites your soul.

Along my journey and even as I make my next move, I have always believed that no matter how hard it is or how long it takes, it's worth pursuing. For most of my life, as far back as I can remember, I never wanted to look back and say,

"I wish I would've, could've" like I've heard so many of my friends, family and other people say. My philosophy on life has been to be conscious about not living life with regrets and not living my life for others. And thus, I gathered up enough energy and courage to fulfill my dream of writing my autobiography.

I wanted to be able to tell my story, in my own words, with hopes of it being an inspiration to others. I hope they find and accept that there is a greater power within themselves and be guided by their intuition, knowing that they too can create the life that they have dreamt of, with no fears or regrets. So here it is: my book, my legacy. As I continue to move forward with this knowing, I'm excited and enthused about taking on this new endeavor, this new chapter in my life.

> **There is a silver lining in everything that we experience**

Our lives are forever evolving and changing with us or without us. When you really think about it, what we do or not do in every moment dictates our next move.

I've been blessed to adhere to the wisdom of God, my mother, mentors and angels throughout my journey. These words of wisdom have shaped and developed my character while instilling in me a strong and unyielding faith that I could achieve anything that I put my mind to.

Each step of the way is a journey unto itself. The lessons that we learned from each experience should help us move forward, provided we remain open to seeing it as an opportunity that shows or guides us to adhere to the message that is being delivered regardless if the experience is good or bad.

There is a silver lining in everything that we experience. It's solely up to us to find it. All we must do is take a step back, remove ourselves from the process and look at the experience with an open mind and not judge it. As espoused by Napoleon Hill, "Every adversity, every failure, every heartache carries with it the seed of an equal or greater benefit." I believe that adversities are what make us.

The adversities that I have experienced have made me stronger and more determined to move forward in my new endeavors. In my new role as a business owner of a Professional Women's Basketball team, author and inspirational speaker, I know that there will be new challenges and adversities that I must endure to succeed. Given my strong faith, determination and willpower, I'm confident that just like before, I will be victorious.

The wonderful thing about this new endeavor is that I will continue to help others by tapping into their natural gifts and abilities. Ultimately, I want to touch every person that I encounter, regardless of their race, color of their skin, ethnicity, gender, socioeconomic status, etc. At the end of the day, I want people to remember how I made them feel. Regardless of their circumstances, I'm committed to help them move forward, if they are willing and have an open mind. To move beyond their challenges, they must be willing to change; otherwise, their efforts will be futile. One must be open, ready and prepared to move forward without fear and trepidation.

No one said that it was going to be easy. Nothing that I earned or accomplished came easy. It was because of my hard work, determination and commitment to do my best in everything that I set out to accomplish. I've had my shares of ups and downs. As Langston Hughes said, "Life for me ain't been no crystal stairs." However, I can tell you from experience that all things are possible if you believe.

Drive and determination alone are what have motivated and inspired me to continue moving forward and not look back. What was done yesterday is what they call history and each day, we are creating history. It's about doing it now. The past is history, the future is not promised, but the present is now. Therefore, all we have is the gift of the present.

Why not make your life worth telling? What will they have said about you? How will you be remembered? I'm mindful that it's not the quantity of your life, but the quality. Some people live a short life and accomplish greatness and some people live a long life, for which many are still here and haven't done anything with their life. These people are just surviving. There is much more to life. And this is what I want people to understand and realize.

Life is short and tomorrow is not promised. We are encouraged to live each day to its fullest. That's why I am so excited and enthused about my next move. I don't believe in wasting time. Time is a precious commodity that we can't get back. You either use it or lose it. Time waits for no one.

As I reflect on my life, there were times when I too didn't value time and as a result, made some unwise decisions that caused me strife. For every cause there is an effect. Everyone has experienced this dilemma and all of us will face this challenge from time to time. Nevertheless, I am grateful that I recognized those moments and consciously made the adjustments. That is why I surged forward to write my book as I make my next move.

Writing this book has been therapeutic and very insightful. It has allowed me to see the patterns of my life, my journey thus far. It's as if I have looked in a mirror or out of a window and witnessed the unfolding of my life. I am reminded of a poem from Shakespeare about how he viewed life while here on earth. "All the world's a stage and all the men and women merely players: they have their exits and their entrances; and one man in his time plays many parts, his acts being seven ages."

As I see this pattern of my life through my own lens, I am encouraged by this revelation, knowing that my next move prepares me for my next move after that, because there is no ending, even after we have passed on.

Life is a continuous flow. I've come to realize that life is symmetrical and not linear. The wonderful thing about life is that we are forever expanding. We are not the same person we were years ago, days ago or even minutes ago. Our bodies and minds are always transforming.

We all came here with a purpose to fulfill and regardless of our circumstances, we must continue to move forward no matter what the challenge is. We might not always find the answers or solutions to our problems or existence, but if we continue to surge forward in the face of adversity, we will survive and hopefully, thrive. What profits a man to gain the whole world but lose his soul in the process?

It's not about how many riches I've accumulated, it's about how much better I would have left the world and did I leave my imprint in this world? I have and hopefully my testimony about how I overcame the challenges in my life and succeeded affirms that everything you desire is possible and you too can leave a legacy for others to follow.

For clarification, please understand that I do believe in enjoying my life while here on earth and plan to live an abundant life. However, I've come to an understanding that I will not allow money and wealth to rule or control me. We came here naked and without any wealth and we will leave the same way. We can't take any of it with us, although many have tried to no avail! Buried with their diamonds and some in their cars.

Life is about the development of our souls, living the highest version of ourselves every moment and I believe ultimately, learning how to love unconditionally. I'm not there yet. However, it is my goal to reach that point before I take my final breath. I still have a lot of growing and plenty of learning ahead of me. As I continue to move forward and make my next move, I will be mindful that in everything that I do, I do it with love, as I remain open and ready for my greatness to expand, leading me to my next move.

It is exciting to know that I still have a lot more to offer to the world. I'm enthused and optimistic about the outcomes of the next chapter in my life. I seek to be better than I was the day before. I look forward to improving the quality of my life every day while helping others along the way. I don't plan for my life to be in vain. Life is a gift and I am grateful for this realization. Although, I don't have a crystal ball and can't predict my future, I'm confident that as I continue to lean on God, the Divine, my life will unfold and speak to the truth of who I am and who I came to be.

I believe that we all came here with a purpose and that is what I believe we should seek every day. Greatness for everyone takes on its own meaning, based on the person's outlook or perspective. Every moment of our lives is an opportunity to pursue our greatness, awakening ourselves and even awakening our children. My goal is to leave a legacy for my children, grandchildren and all of those whose lives I've touched. What is your greatness?

"Go confidently in the direction of your dreams! Live the life you've imagined. As you simplify your life, the laws of the universe will be simpler."
HENRY DAVID THOREAU

VUU Coach Wooten Guided by Legendary Coach "Tricky Tom" Harris

Barvenia Wooten-Cherry '83 poses in front of photo of VUU coach "Tricky Tom" Harris.

Made in the USA
Monee, IL
09 November 2023